Shaolin Kung Fu Online Library

www.kungfulibrary.com

LIAN GONG MI JUE: SECRET METHODS OF ACQUIRING EXTERNAL AND INTERNAL MASTERY

The book was written by Jin Yi Ming in collaboration with Guo Cui Ya. The first edition of the book was issued in August of 1930. The book was printed by the Publishing House Hua Lian in Shanghai.

Chinese Martial Arts - Theory & Practice / Old & Rare Chinese Books, Treatises, Manuscripts

www.shaolinkungfulibrary.com

/Old and Rare Chinese Books in English/

The book covers "external" (WAI GONG) and "internal" (NEI GONG) training methods practiced by traditional schools of the "Shaolin family" (SHAOLIN PAI).

Shaolin Kung Fu Online Library

2024

LIAN GONG MI JUE

SECRET METHODS OF ACQUIRING
EXTERNAL AND INTERNAL MASTERY

Publishing House Hua Lian

Shanghai, 1930

Translated from Chinese

Jin Yi Ming, Guo Cui Ya,
Andrew Timofeevich (Translator)

LIAN GONG MI JUE: Secret Methods of Acquiring External and Internal Mastery

Copyright © Andrew Timofeevich 2007

Translated by Andrew Timofeevich with the participation of Wang Ke Ze and Leonid Serbin. Editor of the translation Andrew Timofeevich.

Book design by Andrew Timofeevich and Olga Akimova.

Published by Shaolin Kung Fu Online Library

USA, 2024

ISBN: 979-8-9919633-1-2

www.shaolinkungfulibrary.com

Disclaimer:

The author and publisher of this material are not responsible in any manner whatsoever for any injury whish may occur through reading or following the instruction in this manual. The activities, physical or otherwise, described in this material may be too strenuous or dangerous for some people, and the reader should consult a physician before engaging in them.

Senior Brother Yi Ming, Master of the Wudang School.

(氏　明　一　金)

"...It is not an idle talk that "Strength can not overcome the Pugilistic Art (Quan Shu), the Pugilistic Art can not overcome Internal Mastery (Gong Fu)". The people think that it is enough to exercise the Pugilistic Art (Quan Shu) but few know that the Pugilistic Art can not withstand the Internal Mastery (Gong Fu) as the Pugilistic Art is sprouts of Gong Fu and Gong Fu itself is the base and root of the Pugilistic Art. There are people who exercise only Gong Fu and do not exercise Quan Shu. But nobody heard that Quan Shu can be exercised without exercising Gong Fu. Such "mastery" is like flying fluff or floating duckweed - too weak base. It is necessary to exercise both Gong Fu and Quan Shu, only in that case there will be a strong base and excellent Mastery."

Jin Yi Ming from Yangzhou. The third decade of August, the 19-th year of the Chinese Republic (1930). Shanghai, province of Jiangsu.

Contents

Part I. WAI GONG
Methods of "External" Training

Hard Gong Fu. Training Methods for Legs and Stances

Hard Gong Fu. Training Methods for Arms and Forearms

Hard Gong Fu. Training Methods for Palms and Fingers

Hard GONG FU. Training Methods for of Pelvis and Shoulders

Hard GONG FU. Method of Successive Blows (PAI DA GONG)

Training Method of External GONG FU from the Book "Canon on Transformation of Muscles and Tendons" (YI JIN JING)

BA DUAN JIN – Eight Pieces of Brocade. Ancient Method of Health Improvement Composed of Eight Exercises

QING GONG. Art of Lightness: the Development of Ability for High and Long Jumps

Part II. NEI ZHUANG XING GONG
Method for Development of Internal Power

***

Foreword by Zhang

In my childhood I went to a private school, liked to challenge boys of my age, often fell down, ignoring pain and bruises. I drove many to tears. Only thanks to morals given to me by my Tutor I realized how dishonorably I had behaved. My schoolmate Jin Yi Ming was older and stronger than I was. He liked to wrestle to test his strength no less than I did. We were like brothers, bosom friends. Of course, I used to bully him but he never showed his superiority over me and other boys, to which I often gave up myself, so the Tutor never punished him. However, each one has one's own way of thinking and judgment. Sometimes a man of courage makes an impression of a timid man and modesty and simplicity, as a rule, are inherent in a man of true intellect. Apparently that is the will of the Almighty. At present we view antiquity like three-year old children view eighty-year olds, and we do not wish to be disappointed. Now, being a grown-up man of high standing, I recall my childhood with some gladness and sorrow. Now everything has changed. Reflection about recent years stirs up uneasiness. However, it is common knowledge that the teaching of Yi Ming on the martial art is in step with the times. Who does not know about the wonderful and miraculous fist of Jin Yi Ming? I read a lot of books on martial arts written by him. "Secret Methods of Internal Training" is the most valuable book. The author expresses himself in the book and the book like a mirror reflects the author. It is especially true in this case – Mastery (Gong Fu) of the author is presented extremely vividly and fully. The author's request to furnish a foreword evoked bygone times in me and I feel some qualm…

6 June of the 19-th year[1] (1930)
Junior disciple Zhang Qing Ling

Editor's notes:

[1] As it was often done in China in the first half of the 20-th century, chronology starts from the Chinese Revolution of 1911.

Author's Preface

The road to power and flourishing (of a state) passes, first of all, through building up people's health. When Russia rattles the saber, when insults come from Japan, when winds are blowing and it is raining over China, descendants of Emperors of Yan and Huang[2], those sick and weak-willed citizens, must acquire such a (combat) technique as to make the country invincible. That is none other than the base for further development as well as a method of counteraction to external interventions. However, it is not an idle talk that he who possesses strength does not match a man in command of the pugilistic art and he who is in command of the pugilistic art can not match a man in command of Gong Fu. The people think that it is enough to exercise the pugilistic art (Quan Shu) but few know that the pugilistic art can not withstand the "internal mastery" (Gong Fu) as the pugilistic art is sprouts of Gong Fu and Gong Fu itself is the base and root of the pugilistic art. There are people who exercise only Gong Fu and do not exercise the pugilistic art. But nobody heard that the pugilistic art can be exercised without exercising Gong Fu. Such "mastery" is like flying fluff or floating duckweed - too weak base. It is necessary to exercise both Gong Fu and Quan Shu, only in that case there will be a strong base and excellent Mastery. It can be said for comparison that if people are strong, a state is strong. Of course, it is necessary to train and teach troops but it would be much more farsighted to start from training and teaching the people (nation). Otherwise, it would be the same thing as exercising the

---

Editor's notes:

[2] Yan Di (abbreviated Yan) and Huang Di (abbreviated Huang), two emperors in ancient Chinese legends, are said to be the earliest ancestors of the Chinese nation.

pugilistic art without exercising Gong Fu – a weak base. If you wish to rule the country, first you must rule your own house. If you wish to rule your own house, you must be capable of ruling yourself. The aim of exercising is not to subjugate (another) man, but to subjugate yourself. If you can subjugate yourself, you will be able to subjugate others as well and be unconquered (by them). If you are able of conquering, others wouldn't dare to conquer you. I have written this book to follow dictates of my conscience. Niu Ti Sheng, Chairman of the Government in the province of Jiangsu and the Chief of "The House of National Martial Art" at the same time, presented me four hieroglyphs – Jiang Guo Zhi Ji – "To strengthen the State is the base of all". We must inspire our four hundred million countrymen for exercising martial arts. If it really happens, if we start seeking for perfection to erase the disgraceful image of "The sick nation of the Eastern Asia", our efforts in the development of the national martial art (Guo Shu) will have the sense.

**The third decade of August, the 19-th year of the Chinese
Republic (1930).
Jin Yi Ming from Yangzhou.
Shanghai, province of Jiangsu.**

Master Jin Yi Ming executes the exercise "Splits in the shape of hieroglyph "One" (一).

Explanations to the exercise "Splits in the shape of hieroglyph "One" (一)"

Split is considered to be a Gong Fu for children, the best thing is to exercise it from young years. I was able to do slits when I was about ten and could tilt the torso to the right and left. Then some break in trainings occurred, therefore now I can do only in such a way: one foot lies flat-wise on the surface and the other foot is arranged vertically (its toe points up). This photo was taken when I was about thirty. If in this position you turn the upper part of your torso to the right, while maintaining feet position unchanged (the right foot is in vertical position, its toe points up, the left foot lies flat-wise on the surface) and set your arms aside to the horizontal position, the split will be in the

shape of hieroglyph "Ten" (+). He who is able to do the split in the shape of hieroglyph (-), as a rule, can do the split in the shape of hieroglyph (+) too. That's why I will not describe the latter separately.

Master Jin Yi Ming is doing the exercise "Iron Bridge".

Rhymed Rule of the Iron Bridge:

"The Iron Bridge" is hard Gong Fu.
The head and feet are on props, the body hangs in the air.
After long training you fill yourself with vital strength and power.
The breast and stomach are strained like a drawn bow.
You are like a steel beam that support a great weight.

General Knowledge about "Internal" and "External", "Soft" and "Hard" Gong Fu

Gong Fu concealed inside a human body is the "internal" Gong Fu and Gong Fu revealed through body extremities is the "external" Gong Fu. The "internal" Gong Fu is opposite to the "external" one like the "soft" Gong Fu is opposite to the "hard" one. It is better to exercise the "internal" Gong Fu than the "external" one. It is better to exercise the "external" Gong Fu than not to exercise at all. Internal mastery is stronger than external one. Though people who attained external mastery certainly much stronger than those who do not exercise at all. Those who exercise see how their health becomes stronger from day to day. Who do not exercise, even if they initially had good health, become weaker from day to day. If the "external" Gong Fu of a man reached a certain level, we can speak about his bravery and courage. If a man achieved success in the "internal" Gong Fu, we can speak about his learning. It is possible to astonish and frighten people with bravery and courage but only learning allows a man to attain the peak of perfection. In that lies the difference between the "internal" and "external" Gong Fu. It is like the difference between a layman and a saint: even if they stand close to each other, they are as far from each other as the sky from the earth.

People know training methods of Ba Duan Jin[3] but do not know wonderful training methods of the "internal" Gong Fu. It is the same as to throw away gold and jade and keep clay and sand. It is tantamount to coming to a treasure house for bricks. However, who actually wishes to get genuine methods for acquiring Gong Fu craves for it like a hungry man for food, like a thirsty man for a drink. It is easy to earn heaps of money but it is difficult to get at least one secret. Everybody has his own way and a true connoisseur reluctantly gives a piece of advice. Even if common interests and aspirations arose, training methods were revealed, a secret recipe passed on, all the same, everything goes like in the proverb: "Useful drug always is bitter"; they retreat in the face of difficulties and stop halfway. Because of it the national heritage perishes. Methods of Gong Fu can and must be promoted and passed on, but one must not flippantly treat that matter. Hard will and commitment are required to learn the "internal" Gong Fu, otherwise there will be one possible result: you will stop halfway and your undertaking fails on the threshold of success. It is imperative to arouse interest; therefore one should start from rather simple and understandable methods to reach great deepness with time. In agreement with above the author explains the "external" Gong Fu first and only then the "internal" Gong Fu. Correspondingly, methods for arms and legs training are given first, then methods

---

Editor's notes:

[3] "Eight Pieces of Brocade", a complex of eight exercises; according to one of the versions was created by marshal Yue Fei (1103-1142) to improve physical training of soldiers; according to other data originates in Shaolin.

for the whole body. The "hard" Gong Fu is treated first, then the "soft" Gong Fu.

The aim of the "hard" Gong Fu is to acquire strength and invincibility and the aim of the "soft" Gong Fu is to acquire flexibility and resilience. Thus, both types of Gong Fu look like being opposite to each other. Therefore, a man exercising the "hard" Gong Fu must not simultaneously exercise the "soft" Gong Fu and vice versa. If a man wants to acquire both "soft" and "hard" Gong Fu, one must not try to achieve both aims at the same time, it should be done in succession. The problem is what to do first. The author thinks the "hard" Gong Fu (mastery) to be improved first, which favors strengthening bone structure, development and reinforcement of muscles and tendons. Then, after reaching a certain level in the "hard" Gong Fu, one may proceed to exercise the "soft" Gong Fu, which leads to higher elasticity of muscles and tendons. Such an approach allows avoiding negative factors that can arise from simultaneous exercising of both types of Gong Fu, a magnificent effect is attainable at that. If a man has really achieved a high level of mastery, he can be hard and soft, tough and flexible. When "hardness" is required, he uses physical force and his hardness is comparable with stone and metal. When "softness" is required, he becomes light and weightless like a hair or feather.

It is thought that it is better to exercise the "soft" Gong Fu in childhood and the "hard" Gong Fu at mature age. As a result of it many who exercised in childhood acquired only the "soft" Gong Fu and did not come close to learning the "hard" Gong Fu. In their turn, many who exercise at mature age focus

attention to "hardness" and ignore "softness". There are few who are in command of both types of Gong Fu. Below we shall give training methods of the "hard" Gong Fu and proceed to the "soft" Gong Fu in the second part of the book.

Part I
WAI GONG
Methods of "External" Training

Jin Yi Ming, Guo Cui Ya. LIAN GONG MI JUE:
Secret Methods of Acquiring External and Internal Mastery (Shanghai, 1930)

Hard Gong Fu.
Training Methods for
Legs and Stances

One should start acquiring the "hard" Gong Fu from leg training. Legs support the whole body. Even if you attained a certain level of mastery but your legs are not trained, the base of your mastery like a tree without roots is not solid. Therefore, one should start from thorough leg training. Below we relate about concrete methods of legs and stances training.

MA DANG BU – Rider's Stance

To take the "Rider's stance" (Ma Dang Bu, or shortly Ma Bu), set feet to sides, point toes forward, bend your legs in knees and squat. Hips must be located horizontally, knees must be on the same vertical with toes. Keep the torso and the neck straight (vertically). Clasp your hands into fists and straighten arms to sides at the shoulder level, the arms position must resemble hieroglyph "One" (➊). Palms centers face down, Hu Kou[4] points forward. Stare forward. You must maintain complete immobility while exercising, do not move arms, lean forward, backward or to sides. The backbone must be vertical, keep the head straight, body weight must be evenly distributed between both legs, feet must press against the ground with the whole sole.

Exercise the stance Ma Bu twice a day – in the morning and evening and count aloud, starting from "one". That way you control the time of being in the stance; at the same time breathing becomes easier[5]. Breathing must be free and natural; one must not hold or speed up one's breath. The time in the stance must be gradually increased. With time you will feel that arms and legs become stronger. After long and persistent exercising you will feel that your feet are as if rooted in the

---

Editor's notes:

[4] HU KOU, lit. "Tiger mouth", here and after a space between the thumb and forefinger.

[5] Counting aloud helps to maintain, what is extremely important, even breathing; it is necessary to count breath ng cycles (breathing in and breathing out) and pronounce number of the cycles while breathing out.

ground and your arms and legs are filled with force. Legs will stand so firm that it will be hard for anybody to push you off your place.

Master Guo Cui Ya demonstrates the stance Ma Bu.

It is imperative to the development of leg strength to exercise the stance Ma Bu. Submerge Qi down, keep the torso vertically, maintain balance. One must not lean to sides, forward or backward.

In spite of apparent simplicity this exercise is very important, one must spend a lot of strength and time to master it. That posture is the best for leg training, so the sound acquisition of Ma Bu is the indispensable condition of the initial stage of training process.

秘 練
訣 功

GONG JIAN BU GONG –
Exercising "Stance of Bow and Arrow"

Training methods for the stance "Bow and Arrow" (Gong Jian Bu) differs from training methods of the "Rider's" stance (Ma Bu). When exercising Ma Bu, it is necessary to maintain complete immobility, any movements are not allowed – it is a static training. On the contrary, exercising Gong Jian Bu is a dynamic exercise which includes punching, torso turning, swiftness and mobility of the whole body is developed at that.

The posture for training is the following: set feet forward and back in order the distance between them to be equal to a big step. The front leg is bent in knee and the back leg is straight. Toes of both feet point forward and a little aside (obliquely), feet are parallel to each other. The shin of the bent (front) leg must be vertical. Usually this position is called "Bow in front, Arrow behind" (Qian Gong Hou Jian) but there are other names too. If the left leg is in front it is called "Left bow, right arrow" (Juo Gong Yu Jian"). If the right leg is in front it is called "Right bow, left arrow (Yu Gong Juo Jian). The common name of the position is Gong Jian Bu – "Position of Bow and Arrow". The hands are clenched into fists, the arms are bent in elbows, the elbows are moved back so that fists to be near the waist, palm centers point upward.

Master Guo Cui Ya in the position "Left bow, right arrow"

After taking the initial position, proceed to training. If your left leg is bent and located in front, punch with the right fist forward (the arm straightens horizontally at the shoulder level; while punching, the fists turns with the palm center downward). Then turn to the right side (for example, if in the beginning you stood facing east, you must turn to 180 degrees with the face to west; for that shift body weight a little to the front parts of feet, raise a little bit heels and turn to the right, the front parts of feet being axes of rotation). While turning, the right fist that

punched before returns to the initial position near the waist with palm center turned upward. At the same time the left arm straightens to the right; while taking the right Gong Bu, the left fist punches to the right (straight arm, the fist at the shoulder level with its center facing down). Turn in such a way alternately to the left and right, taking the position "Bow and Arrow" and making one punch after another.

Master Guo Cui Ya in the position "Right bow, left arrow".

At first one must not exercise to the point of exhaustion. At the first stage, it is important to keep up with correctness of stances

and blows, so it is not worth hurrying. It is necessary to increase gradually the load – number of repetitions, speed and strength of blows. With time arms and legs will become stronger, deftness and swiftness in punching and torso turning will develop.

Jin Yi Ming, Guo Cui Ya. LIAN GONG MI JUE:
Secret Methods of Acquiring External and Internal Mastery (Shanghai, 1930)

Red Child Worships Goddess Guan Yin

Master Guo Cui is doing the exercise "A red child worships goddess Guan Yin".

Stand upright with feet together. Raise one leg forward up to the horizontal position (straight leg), the foot toe points up. The other leg stands steady, it toe is turned outside (a firm toe and heel position and the knee a little bent are three constituent parts of position steadiness). Fold arms in front of the breast

(like Buddhists fold palms as a token of greeting and adoration, finger tips point up). The arms are bent in elbows in front of the breast, finger tips are at the shoulder level. The torso is straight, stare forward, do not lower your head. After taking the above position, bend the supporting leg and move down. Then unbend the supporting leg and slowly rise up. Try to keep the leg that is stretched forward horizontal, do not bend the knee. Move down and rise up again. It should be done many times. With time leg strength will increase manifold.

Master Guo Cui is doing the exercise "A red child worships goddess Guan Yin".

Jin Yi Ming, Guo Cui Ya. LIAN GONG MI JUE:
Secret Methods of Acquiring External and Internal Mastery (Shanghai, 1930)

At first this exercise may seem very difficult to do and may be you will be able only to squat (on one leg) but will not be able to rise up or will be able to squat and rise up only one time or even not able to stand on one leg. But if you exercise persistently from day to day, with time you will be able to do this exercise easily. Leg strength will increase with higher loads. If by exercising both legs in turn you will be able to bring number of repetitions up to hundred times, your legs will get tremendous strength. If you encounter an enemy who acquired high mastery, he will not be able to endure even one of your kicks.

秘 練
訣 功

Striking One Leg at the Other

Master Guo Cui is doing the exercise "Striking one leg at the
other".

Kick with the instep of the back feet at the lower part of the shin
of the front leg, behind, at the ankle level. Step forward in turn
with both legs. Keep the torso vertical, do not sway. With time
legs are filled with force. You will always win prize places in
races.

秘 練
訣 功

Take the stance "at attention". Place hands on the waist (Hu Kou points up, the thumb is behind, the other four fingers are in front). Make a step forward with the left leg, put down the left feet to the ground, make a strong kick with the instep of the right foot at the back part of the left shin at the ankle level[6] (i.e. at the place where laces are tied on the lower part of the trouser-leg). Then, without putting down the right foot to the ground, make a step with the right leg forward. After putting the right foot on the ground, make a strong kick with the instep of the left foot at the back part of the right shin at the ankle level. In such a way, stepping with the right and left leg in succession, you kick with the instep of the back leg at the back part of the ankle joint of the front leg. It is necessary to exercise daily. With time your legs will stand firmly like piles dug into the ground. If you wish to strengthen your legs considerably you should not ignore this exercise.

Editor's notes:

[6] That is actually means that the kick is done at the Achilles tendon.

Jin Yi M ng, Guo Cui Ya. LIAN GONG MI JUE:
Secret Methods of Acquiring External and Internal Mastery (Shanghai, 1930)

Hard Gong Fu.
Training Methods for
Arms and Forearms

Striking with Forearms and Elbows

A part of an arm from a wrist to an elbow has a hard and solid bone, therefore it suits well for exercising the hard Gong Fu. As far as the wrist is concerned, it is a less solid part of the arm, especially of its inner part. It is comparatively easy to train the outer part of a wrist and much more difficult the inner one, but certainly it is necessary to train the inner part of a wrist, one can not do without it. One must train oneself consistently and persistently and in some time the strength of the inner side of a wrist will not be inferior to that one of the outer side.

The training method is as follows. Take a stand beside a pole that supports the house roof. Strike at the pole with both forearms in succession, with both outer and inner parts. Raise the right forearm to the right and up and strike at the pole with the inner part of the forearm, then move the right arm to the left side and strike at the pole with the outer side of the forearm. Then do the same with the left arm. Move from the elbow to the wrist and back in such a way to harden the forearm on the whole length. You should not strike hard at first, you may simply push the pole. Increase number and strength of blows

gradually. With time your arms become strong and the pole start shaking under your blows. Proceed to trainings with trees after it. Choose a tree with smooth rind that is not too thick at first and go on training persistently. With time the tree will start trembling from your blows and start withering. Then, proceed to a thicker tree. Your forearms will ultimately become as hard as stone or metal. If you strike at an ordinary (untrained) man, you will inevitably cause bone fracture and a rupture of tendons in him. If you strike at a tree, it will tremble. Only keep in mind that you should not hasten to get results in Gong Fu training; to exercise persistently and not from time to time, this is the most important; in that case mastery will be excellent.

Training methods for elbows on the whole is identical to training methods for forearms. Blows at a pole or a tree must also be made. One must only keep in mind that the region of an elbow consists of three parts. They are the lower part of the elbow (on the forearm), the upper part of the elbow (on the shoulder) and the tip of the elbow. Three parts of the elbow are used to deliver different kinds of blows but the training methods (hardening) for them are the same. The tip of the elbow is used for powerful blows with great piercing force and the lower and upper parts of the elbow are used to deliver powerful "splitting" blows. Many think that is enough to train only one (usually the right) elbow. However, it is better to train both elbows, as arms and elbows are most often used in a real hand-to-hand combat. In order to overwhelm an experienced enemy, one must certainly have two trained arms and elbows. Results of persistent training will always be needed and here everything unexceptionally depends on will of iron and tenacious commitment of a trainee.

Jin Yi Ming, Guo Cui Ya. LIAN GONG MI JUE:
Secret Methods of Acquiring External and Internal Mastery (Shanghai, 1930)

Striking at Sand Bags

Training in blows at a sand bag not only increases the strength of arms but also improves mobility and flexibility of torso and legs. It might be said that it is one of the best methods to perfect one's skills in the hard Gong Fu. During the first stage, hang a bag filled with sand and small pebbles on a beam indoors or on a tree. The weight of the bag and proportion of sand and pebble must be selected individually according to your physical development. The bag must hang approximately at the breast level of the trainee. Each day, in the morning and evening, one must strike different kinds of blows at the bag with both arms in any sequence you like: with palms, fists, elbows, forearms. The blows must not be too strong at first in order to avoid body damage. Blow strength must be increased with arm strengthening. With time the bag will start swinging under your blows. As soon as the bag makes a swing to your side, it is necessary to make an immediate punch or strike with another part of your arm, not letting the bag to approach you. Blows must be hailed one after another, from the left and right, like rain drops, without interruption. With time arms will become strong and then some sand or pebbles may be added in the bag. Train yourself in such a way again, trying to attain continuous, strong and well-aimed blows. Increase gradually the weight of the bag and its hardness (the proportion of sand and pebbles in the bag) with the growth of your strength and mastery.

With time you will feel that you are able to do the exercise easily, that means that one bag already is not enough. In that

case you hang beside one more sand bag. Usually the distance between the bags is about 7–8 CHIs[7], but it may differ, depending on the length of ropes for bags and the dimension of your training site. Training methods are similar: take a stand between the two bags and strike at them in succession, keeping both bags at some distance and not letting them to approach you. Here you must use your fists, palms, elbows, and forearms, depending on the distance to the bag, its speed and the position in regard to you. When you learn to deal with two bags freely, you may hang the third bag at an equal distance from two others (that means the bags are located in a triangle pattern). Take a stand in the middle of the triangle formed by the bags and train yourself as above described. The only difference is like that: in the previous case (two bags) you struck on each bag in turn, now no sequence is observed, a blow is made at the bag which is the nearest to you at the present moment. If you haven't got enough time to beat off a bag with fist or arm, resort to kicking. You must act swiftly and adroitly - the bags must not get in touch with your torso or head.

Having acquired the exercise with three bags, add the fourth one. Now the bags must hang on sides of a square and you stand in its center so the bags will be in front, back, on the right and left. The training methods remain to be the same. If you acquire this kind of Gong Fu well, you, even attacked by several enemies at the same time and from different directions, can

---

Editor's notes:

[7] CHI, a Chinese measure of length approximately equal to 1/3 m (33 cm), or 1.094 ft. The distance between bags is about 2.3 m (7.66 ft) to 2.6 m (8.75 ft).

successfully defend yourself and will not give them a chance to approach you. This kind of Gong Fu is usually acquired for practical use.

秘 練
訣 功

Pulling a Hanging Sand Bag

Training methods for "Pulling a hanging sand bag" is as follows. One should fill a bag made of canvas with some sand and small stones (pebbles or gravel). Bag weight depends on your physical capabilities when you start training. Hang up the bag by a cord on an indoor beam, at the level of your breast approximately. Arrange a pulley on the beam. Take the second cord and lay it over the pulley. Tie one of the ends to the neck of the hanging bag, tie a small cloth ball to the second end of the cord for convenience of catching by hand. Take a stand beside the bag in the position Gong Bu ("Bow in front, arrow behind"). Place one of the hands on your waist, move the second one forward and seize the cloth ball at the end of the cord. Pull the cord down and toward you, causing the bag to start rising up. If the left leg is in front, pull the bag with your right hand; if the right leg is in front, pull with your left hand. Draw the arm toward you, then return it to the initial position slowly. The bag will return to the initial lower position. Then pull toward you again and so on, until you exhaust. Change the stance after that and pull the bag with the other hand.

It is necessary to train oneself in similar way twice a day, in the morning and evening. With growth of arms strength, bag weight and number of exercise repetitions should be gradually increased. Alongside with the above-mentioned position Gong Bu, you can also exercise in the position Ma Bu ("Rider's stance"). In that case you take a stand with your side facing the bag and pull the bag with the cord. The stance must be maintained stable and firm and the position of legs and torso unchanged. When you attain mastery in that exercise, you will

be able to pull even a big and heavy man and he will tumble down like a rotten tree.

Master Liang Zu Rung is doing the exercise "Pulling a hanging sand bag".

There is an iron hook above, over which a cord tied to the bag is laid. A small bamboo handle is tied to the other end of the cord. During a training session one must hold the handle and pull the cord. In that way arms strength increases. The photo shows a training method somewhat different from that one described in the text but the essence of the matter is the same.

Jin Yi Ming, Guo Cui Ya. LIAN GONG MI JUE:
Secret Methods of Acquiring External and Internal Mastery (Shanghai, 1930)

Bandying Sand Bags

This exercise requires bags different from that ones for the exercise "Striking at sand bags", a training method is also different. First, here the size and weight of bags is smaller. Second, this exercise is not individual but a group one: the group can be of 2-3 men up to 4-5 men. At the initial stage bag weight usually is about 10 JINs (5 kg or 11 lb) but it may be more or less, depending on the physical condition of a trainee. If even number of men participates, they form two subgroups and line up opposite each other. The distance between the subgroups is selected depending on the training level of participants. Initially the first group throws bags, the second one catches them, then vice versa, the second throws, the first one catches and so on. In such a way they bandy bags, evenly training the left and right arms. That work can be complicated with higher growth of training level: bags are thrown in any sequence, at different heights and at different angles. Here some dexterity and skill are required: one must move forward and backward to catch a flying bag. One can also throw a bag to any member of the opposite group; that introduces the element of unexpectedness, develops peripheral vision and the ability of visual control over the situation around. The weight of bags must be gradually increased, arms strength will grow respectively. In the process of such training mobility and dexterity increase, coordination (mutual work) of arms, legs, torso, and eyes improve, strength and endurance increase. If you simultaneously improve the pugilistic skills (fighting techniques) you will be able to attain a rather high level of mastery.

Exercising with a Stone Padlock

Exercising with a stone padlock is special exercises to develop arm strength, strengthening elbows, shoulders and wrists. The stone padlock is a stone gymnastic tool in the shape a padlock where an upper "shackle" serves as a handle. There is a great deal of methods for training with the stone padlock. Initially one should do so: set one arm against your side, firmly squeeze the "shackle" of the padlock with the other arm and raise it above your head. Raise the padlock at first with the method of "pushing", that is in one movement from the floor to the position above the head with the straight arm. Then, when muscles become strong, do it in two steps: at first raise the padlock to your shoulder with the arm bent and the elbow pressed to your side. Then, push the padlock up above your head. Initially you may help yourself with legs and torso movements, with time when arms become stronger you must raise the padlock, using only arms force without straining legs and torso muscles. Later, it is necessary to proceed from the "pushing" to the method of "press", i.e. to raise the padlock slowly and lower it slowly.

After acquiring the previous exercise, proceed to more complicated ones. For instance, stretch the arm with the padlock forward or to a side in the horizontal plane and return it to the breast. Or stretch the arm and stop, gradually increasing the time of staying in that position. Further, it is necessary to throw the padlock up, at that one arm throws, the other arm catches and vice versa. More complex variant of that exercise is juggling with the padlock. At that the padlock can make one, two or even more turns, depending on the height to which it is

秘　練
訣　功

thrown. It is possible to develop the arms strength equal to 1000 JINs in such a way[8].

Editor's notes:

[8]JIN, a Chinese measure of weight equal to 0.5 kg (1.102 lb) approximately.

Exercising with a Stone Yoke

Methods for exercising with a stone yoke (barbell) are almost the same as methods for a stone padlock. Only exercises with a stone padlock are done with each arm in turn and a stone yoke (barbell) is usually held with both arms. The usual weight of a stone yoke is two, three or even four times bigger than that one of a stone padlock. Usually the weight of a stone yoke is within 100-160 JINs (50-80 kg or 110-176 lb), but the final choice of the weight depends on your physical conditions.

The stone yoke consists of two stone disks with holes in the center where a strong bamboo pole is inserted. The training method is as follows: take a stand in front of the barbell, opposite the middle part of the pole (the bar); part your feet to the left and right to a distance of one step. Lean over and grasp the pole (the bar) with both hands (palms are turned toward you, thumbs are turned to face each other). The distance between your hands must be about 1-2 CHIs (33-66 cm or 1.094-2.188 ft). Raise up the barbell to the breast with a jerk, at the same time straighten legs and take the vertical position. Make a pause. At that moment elbows of both arms are pressed to your sides with palms facing up, the insides of wrists point forward. Tilt the torso a little back and strain stomach muscles, maintain the stable position. Straighten arms and push the barbell up above your head and then return to the initial position to your shoulders. If you feel that you have enough strength, push the barbell once more, if not, put them down to the floor. This exercise must be done each day. Try to raise and put down the beam at least several times. With time strength of arms will increase and you will be able to raise the barbell with one arm.

**Master Wan Hou An is exercising with a stone yoke, holding it
on his head.
"You shift legs to follow the rotation of the torso.
The stone yoke rotates to follow head turns.
The yoke rotates on the head – it is incomparable and
unsurpassed mastery." /Jin Yi Ming/**

Exercising with barbell demands good coordination of all parts
of the body; while exercising the body must be mobile and the
legs quick. It is necessary to control the position of your body's
center of gravity and the position of the barbell all the time,
otherwise in case of the smallest negligence a danger of
damaging your body arises. It is better for a physically strong

man to exercise with barbell and for a less strong one with a stone padlock or a stone for five fingers (see below), it is easy and useful.

Master Yang Dian Bang is exercising with a stone yoke, supporting it with one bent arm located in the horizontal plane on the shoulder level. The weight of the barbells is about 150 JINs (75 kg or 165 lb). Master Yang says that he does not need to apply great efforts to do this exercise. Today he had to maintain this position longer time to take a photo; however, judging by that how easy he stood, he almost was not conscious that the stone yoke was heavy, he felt easy and free.

Master Wu Xi Liang during a training session. The barbell are held on elbows.

It is easy to raise barbell up but it is not so simple to lower it, therefore we recommend choosing sufficiently light barbell at first. One must lower the barbell, grasping them with hands by its bar, at first with one hand, then with the other. One may catch the bar of the barbell with both hands at the same time, but it is more difficult variant. One must not thoughtlessly try it without understanding the essence of the matter.

秘 練
訣 功

Master Wu Xi Liang during a training session. The stone yoke
is raised with one hand.

If you make your barbell swing with the force of the wrist, it is
called "Lotus leaves sway in the wind" (FENG PIAO HE YE).
If you toss up your barbell with your left arm and catch it up
with your right arm, this method is called "Deity passes the
bridge" (XIAN REN GUO JIAO). It is difficult to capture those
movements; therefore we decided to make only a description.

Jin Yi Ming, Guo Cui Ya. LIAN GONG MI JUE:
Secret Methods of Acquiring External and Internal Mastery (Shanghai, 1930)

Exercising with a Stone Grasped with Five Fingers

The essence of the method is as follows: take a stone weighing about 10 JINs (5 kg or 11 lb) or more or less, depending on your physical capabilities. Ask a stone-cutter to do so that the stone will have the shape of a disc with smooth and flat upper and lower sides. It is necessary to chisel five hollows 7-8 FENs[9] (2.31-2.64 cm or 0.92-1.05 in) deep in the upper sides of the stone. Relative position of the hollows is so that it would be convenient to grasp with five fingers slightly spread. Part your feet to the left and right at the distance of one step, bend legs in knees, take Ma Bu stance. Place one of the hand on the waist and grasp a stone with five fingers of the other hand. Concentrate force in fingertips, raise up the stone to the breast level. Turn the hand with back down and fingers up, the lower surface of the stone will point up and the surface with holes for fingers down respectively. The arm remains slightly bent in elbow. Let the stone down to the groin level, turn it with the side with holes up and raise it again to the breast level. Exercise both arms in turn several times. It is necessary to exercise each day in the morning and evening. While exercising, the number of lifting and lowering movements must be counted; increase that number gradually. This method is significantly easier as compared with exercising with a stone yoke.

Editor's notes:

[9] FEN, a unit of length equal to 0.33 cm or 0.1312 in.

秘 練
訣 功

**Master Jin Yi Ming is exercising with a stone grasped with five
fingers.**

Five hollows for five fingers have been chiseled in the stone.
Raise the stone up, firmly holding it in fingers. Turn the stone
upside down, so its lower side will be in the horizontal plane.
Return the stone to the initial position and repeat the movement
after a short pause. With time the wrist will acquire required
flexibility and force.

Master Jin Yi Ming is exercising with a stone grasped with five fingers.

He makes his wrist flexible by practicing his arm. It is necessary to turn the stone over many times in succession. After training for a long time the stone will seem light like a head of cabbage.

Hard GONG FU. Training Methods for Palms and Fingers

Hardening of the Palms with a Sand Bag

Training method for palms with a sand bag is as follows. Take a bag made of canvas and fill it with sand. The weight of the bag and its size is decided upon by a trainee himself. Usually the length of the bag is about 1.5 CHIs (0.5 m, or 1.64 ft), the width is about 8 CUNs[10] (26.7 cm, or 10.5 in), the diameter of a bag filled with sand is a little more than 4 CUNs (13.3 cm, or 5.25 in) respectively. Put the sand bag on a bench or a stone footstep in the yard. Each day, early in the morning and before going to bed, you strike at the bag. The exercise is divided into three parts. The first part: delivering chopping blows with the edge of the palm, that is, with the place from the wrist to the little finger. The second part: striking with the back of the hand. The

---

Editor's notes:

[10] CUN, a Chinese unit of length, equal to about 3.33 cm, or 1.312 inches.

third part: striking with a palm (with the whole surface). You strike in the above-mentioned sequence, changing hands. One should not apply excessive efforts initially; training intensity must be increased gradually. After 100 days of uninterrupted training a sand bag may be replaced with a big stone.

Hardening of the Palms with a Stone

Training methods for palms with a stone are the same like those ones for palms on a sand bag. It is necessary to practice hands in turn, increasing force and number of blows gradually. If you start training with a stone from the very beginning, you can feel rather strong sensation of pain. Therefore it is desirable to strengthen the palms with a sand bag at first. In principle, it is possible to start practicing the side surface of a palm (from the wrist to the little finger) and the palm itself with a stone; a good result can be reached in such a way even quicker (if one does not forget about caution). In that case, if you try to strike at a sand bag, it will seem to you too soft to withstand your blow. At the same time muscles of the back of the hands are not so strong as those ones of the metacarpus and the palm, that's why if you strike a little harder at a stone, immediate sensation of pain arises. Taking into account the above-said, probably it is better to start exercising with a sand bag and then proceed to a stone. After all, everything depends on your choice. The author of the book trained himself in his childhood with a stone and in this connection such a happening came to his mind. Once I

came to my friend who used a sand bag for exercising. I made an attempt to strike a few blows and felt that the bag was too soft and it could not withstand my blows. Just keep in mind that it must be daily training. If some day for some reasons a man misses training, he feels itch in the metacarpus and in palms. It means that training has become a strong habit. Irrespective of your training means – a bag or a stone, you can repel the enemy and be ready for any unexpected events if you train yourself hard every day during three years.

Hardening of the Fingers with a Sand Bag

Training methods for fingers, though diverse they are, come to blows at a stone or a brick in the end. One can practice one finger (forefinger) separately, two fingers (forefinger and middle finger), three fingers (forefinger, middle finger and fourth finger) as well as four or five fingers together. In finger practicing, they single out fingertips strengthening, strengthening joints between the second and third phalanx and strengthening sides of fingers. Fingertips and joints between the second and third phalanx are practiced to make "piercing" blows, including blows at acupuncture points. Sides of forefingers and middle fingers are practiced to do "knocking" blows. Skin and bones of fingers are not strong enough; therefore, they must be strengthened through prodding a sand bag with them. The method is as follows: take a sand bag and lay it on a bench. It is possible to exercise while standing or

sitting. Hold the bag open with the aid of one hand, press the thumb of the other hand to the side of the palm, close the other four fingers and straighten them. Nails of fingers must be trimmed. Bend slightly and strain fingertips and prod them in sand. Do this exercise with two hands in turn. Two or three training sessions must be conducted every day, during a training session a certain number of prods must be done. Increase force and number of blows gradually. Fingers become strong. After three months sand may be gradually replaced with small stones (pebbles). When sand is fully replaced with pebbles, one may proceed to exercising with a brick or a stone. The most important thing: one must exercise daily. Here the level of mastery exclusively depends on persistence of a trainee. If you do exercising diligently, with time you will obtain a good result; that is indisputable truth.

Simplified Finger Training

While exercising fingers, special attention must be given to fingertips, as such main technical actions as squeezing, grasping, prodding are done just precisely with fingertips. The simplified finger strengthening is as follows: bend the thumb and little finger, straighten and closely link up your forefinger, middle finger and fourth finger. Nails must be closely trimmed. Bend three stretched fingers a little so that their tips will be at the same level. Strain three fingers and prod a table, chair, stool, wall etc. with them, always and everywhere when circumstances allow to do it. One can exercise everywhere: while walking, sitting or even lying; it is possible to prod your own leg or

shoulder. Other kinds of training need ground, time and place, equipment after all. In this case everything is much simpler: you can exercise without interrupting daily routine. If you daily exercise during three years, with the aid of three fingers you can resist any enemy.

Jin Yi Ming, Guo Cui Ya. LIAN GONG MI JUE:
Secret Methods of Acquiring External and Internal Mastery (Shanghai, 1930)

Strengthening Fingers with Potion

There are some people who strengthen their fingers with potion. That method is called YING ZHAO SHOU – "The hand of eagle's claws". The potion includes the following ingredients: pounded legs of two birds, crumbled-up elephant hide (3 LIANs[11]), shell of the pangolin (3 LIANs), BANG XIA – roasted roots of Pinellia ternata (3 LIANs), Sichuan poisonous plant CHUAN WU TOU (3 LIANs), poisonous plant CAO WU TOU (3 LIANs). Mix all the above-mentioned components and soak them in ginger juice, then add into the potion six of the following components: DAN GUI (Chinese angelica), plant called WA SONG, PI XIAO (Glauber's salts), plant TOU GU CAO, ZI HUA DI DING (Viola patrini), table salt - 3 LIANs each.

Put everything into a pot, pour 5 JINs (2.5 kg, or 5.51 lb) of seasoned Chinese vinegar and 6 JINs (3 kg, or 6.61 lb) of river water. Every day, in the morning and evening, put the pot on slow fire and dip your hands into it. When the potion reaches hot state take your hands out of the pot and let them dry without wiping them. Bend and unbend fingers with force until they are able to bend and unbend free, without effort. That method is also called WU LONG ZHAO – "Black Dragon's claws". With time force will concentrate in fingertips and QI penetrate tendons and bones.

Editor's notes:

[11] LIAN, a Chinese measure of weight, equivalent of 50 g, or 1.764 oz.

**Master Jin Yi Ming is practicing his fingers, using the method
"Black dragon's claws".**

**Collect force in fingertips, bend and unbend fingers slowly with
force. Repeat like that many times.**

In everyday life the hands look like the ones of ordinary people,
but when it is needed, the hands will become as hard as metal or
stone. If you strike a straight blow with four straightened fingers
linked together, you are able to pierce a side of a bull. And if
you deliver a chopping blow with your palm, you will cut off the
head of a bull. In days of old some wandering knight called

Wang Yi Zhua lived to the north of the river of Huanghe. He trained himself according to those methods and attained great success. If he caught a man, the man felt as if steel hooks had hooked up him. For that the knight was nicknamed "King of eagle's claw". Due to the fact that the effect of potion reaches marrow, the strength of fingers and the hands reaches unbelievable value. By this, the method differ from others and therefore are the most effective.

Master Jin Yi Ming is practicing his fingers, using the method "Black dragon's claws".

Palm of Tiger's Claw

Practicing palm of the tiger's claw consists in the following. Spread five fingers and set their tips against horizontal or vertical surface (table, wall etc.). Concentrate force in the wrist; fingers and the wrist must be strained. Bend five fingers and press them to edges of the palm, at the same time strike at a wall with the metacarpus. Then, straighten fingers and prod the wall with them again, at the same time breathe in. Strike at the wall with the metacarpus while breathing out. Continue according to the above-described method: prod fingers while breathing in and strike (with the metacarpus) while breathing out. While breathing in, concentrate force and relax, while breathing out direct stream of force into the palm. There also are special potions for that method, they can increase training efficiency. In that case dip your hands into the hot potion, take them out and let them dry without wiping. Then "prod" and "spank" as described above. With time all five fingers and wrist will become as strong as claws of a tiger. It is a very effective training method for fingers and wrists.

Jin Yi Ming, Guo Cui Ya. LIAN GONG MI JUE:
Secret Methods of Acquiring External and Internal Mastery (Shanghai, 1930)

Finger, Golden Needle

When somebody speaks about practicing one finger he usually uses the term "Finger, golden needle". Meantime, the Shaolin School uses its own term – "Diamond finger". When two fingers are practiced, it is called "Fingers, golden scissors". Practicing three fingers is called "Pilfering fingers" or "Fingers, tripod". Four fingers are "Fingers, golden scoop". Monk Yi Guang was the most outstanding among those who acquired the method "Finger, golden needle". He was born in the province of Yunnan, in his childhood he often went to Zhejiang and Hangzhou together with his farther. After his farther died he got a job as a servant in the family of an official. When he grew up he ran away to the Shaolin monastery where he, blessed by His Reverence Jiu Ye Yuan, made a monk's vow. He was so physically weak that he could not exercise together with monks. So he did breathing exercises. Hardly half a year passed as he became much stronger. Yi Guang was of great enterprising spirit. After some time he was sent as the superior of the temple Jin Yun. He practiced one finger (forefinger) every morning and evening. With time Yi Guang attained unimaginable skills. If his finger pressed on a man's body even through several layers of boards, all the same the man felt pain. If he pressed stronger, a bruise appeared, if still stronger – the man felt acute and unbearable pain. One should devote his life to this wonderful art to obtain such a result; otherwise such a peak (of mastery) is unattainable.

Master Jin Yi Ming is showing the method "Finger like a golden needle".

Set two forefingers against a wall, put feet as far from the wall as possible. Your arms are perpendicular to the wall, the wrists are straight. Stay on tiptoe. The forefingers are strengthened in such a way.

Training method is as follows. Each day one must carry out six training sessions. Set tips of your forefingers against the wall, put your feet back, lean the torso forward and stand tiptoe. Forefinger, wrist and whole arm must be on one straight line

perpendicular to wall surface. Initially a torso tilt may be equal to 20-30 degrees and it is quite tangible load. Gradually, as fingers strengthen, feet must be put farther and farther from the wall and torso tilt increased. It is a very long process: one must train oneself during thirty years. After some time add the following exercise: lie down prone on the ground, set both forefingers and toes against the ground. Straighten arms and raise up the body above the ground. Only two forefingers and ten toes should support you. Bend and unbend arms with raising and lowering the torso. After training for a long time forefingers will become like steel bars. You can bend and unbend your arms several dozen times without feeling tiredness or pain. It means you have reached perfection in that kind of GONG FU.

Hard GONG FU. Training Methods for Pelvis and Shoulders

Exercise "Pushing with the Pelvis"

This exercise is to train the ability to make strong pushes with the side surface of the body between a leg and the waist. The bone in this place is hard and massive, it suits well for practicing the hard GONG FU. The method is as follows: take a stand sideways near wall, pole or tree at a distance of a few CUNs[12]. Make a push against the wall, pole or tree with the side of the pelvis. If you execute a push with the right side of the pelvis, bend the right arm and press it to the left side of the breast; if you train the left side, bend and press the left arm to the right side of the breast. Practice both sides of the pelvis in turn, changing arms position respectively. It is necessary to be in training two or three times each day, number and force of pushes must be gradually increased. At first, excessive efforts should not be made. With time pelvis bones will become stronger and the force of a push will be significantly greater. Finally, a thick brick wall can crush down with your push and

---

Editor's notes:

[12] One CUN is equal to 3.33 cm, or 1.312 in.

the attacking enemy can be pushed away to several ZHANGs[13]. However, it is necessary to master this method well to reach that.

Exercise "Pushing with Shoulder"

Practicing the shoulder is different from practicing the pelvis only in the place of force application but the methods are the same. One can also exercise indoors near wall, or outdoors near tree or pole. Do exercising several times a day. With time the force of a push will be significantly greater. While exercising, it is necessary to lean the head in order not to hit it by accident. If you push with your right shoulder, clench the right hand into fist and move it back a little and move the right shoulder forward. Lean the head to the left a little, look at the right shoulder, strike with the right shoulder at wall, pole or tree. It is advisable to practice both the right and left shoulders. It is not recommended to practice only one shoulder: the less untrained spots, the less weaker spots.

Editor's notes:

[13] ZHANG, a Chinese measure of length, equivalent of 3.33 m, or 3.645 yd approximately.

Jin Yi Ming, Guo Cui Ya. LIAN GONG MI JUE:
Secret Methods of Acquiring External and Internal Mastery (Shanghai, 1930)

Hard GONG FU. Method of Successive Blows (PAI DA GONG)

Eight point instruction on the use of the method PAI DA GONG

1. Purpose and destination of exercising PAI DA GONG

In ancient times, alongside with training, different auxiliary actions were done, for instance, swallowing paper with magic exorcism. Certainly, it is a superstition. Mysticism aside, the essence of the method is as follows: strengthen the whole body in order to turn it from a weak into strong and healthy body, in order a sickly man to become strong and robust. As our ancestors said, train your own body so that it would be invulnerable to swords and spears. But now a lot of firearms are available, their killing capacity by far exceeds age-old broadswords, spears, swords, and halberds. It would seem to be senseless to exercise. However, such exercising additionally enables a man excellent health. If you persistently exercise during three years, your body can not yet safely withstand powerful blows of broadswords and spears, but in a hand-to-hand combat you are quite able to win even if your enemy uses

秘 練
訣 功

cold steel. Being in command of this kind of GONG FU, you will always be able to repel an attack and defend yourself, in that lies its original purpose.

2. Aids used in the practice of PAI DA GONG

At the initial training stage when muscles and bones are not strong enough, it is necessary to use a wooden brick (piece of wood), 1 CUN (3.33 cm, or 1.312 in) thick and 7 or 8 CUNs (23.3-26,6 cm, or 9.18-10.5 in) long. You must strike with it at four body extremities, breast, sides, stomach, back and head as described below. With time, when the body becomes stronger, one may use a clay brick or a heavier wooden pestle. Some time later, a smooth stone or an iron pestle may be used.

3. While practicing PA DA GONG, a yell (a breath-out), QI and internal effort (force) must be synchronized

When practicing with a brick for striking, all instructions must be strictly followed. It is very important. Otherwise you will do harm to your health, not to mention success. Blows struck improperly or too strong blows beyond the physical conditions of a trainee can cause body damages. A timely breath-out (yell), QI and inner effort need special care. Coordination of three of those components is the key to success. When you strike at some part of the body you must loudly count (scream out)

number of blows: "one" (**yi**) – "two" (**er**), "three" (**san**). It is necessary to concentrate attention on the trained part of the body and see to that a yell and internal effort arises simultaneously at the moment when the brick touches the trained part of the body. Never tolerate non-synchronized actions. Internal effort (muscles strain) must correspond to external force and arise exactly at the striking moment. Concentration of attention at the spot under blows and muscle relaxation of the trained region at the time between blows cause the inflow of QI and blood there. So strengthening of body parts is attained and only in such a way some progress in training can be made.

4. Time of training

Usually exercising is done twice a day: in the morning and in the evening. The most suitable time is sunrise and sunset. Some do so: they rise up at 4 or 5 o'clock in the morning and exercise one time a day. That may be done so. It is a trainee who decides.

5. Warming up exercises before exercising PAI DA GONG

Before exercising, warming up exercises for body extremities must be done. Otherwise body damages are possible during a training session, which contradicts to training purposes. At first it is necessary to shake arms and legs, then do any exercises or

秘 練
訣 功

run. It not only increases the flexibility and mobility of extremities but relaxes muscles, activates breathing, improves blood circulation as well. One must always keep it in mind.

6. Procedure of practicing body parts and number of blows

A. Both arms (comprising the upper and lower parts and elbow).

B. Both legs (comprising the front part of the shin and the surface of the hip).

C. Breast (comprising the left and right side).

D. Sides (comprising the left and ride sides).

E. Back.

F. Stomach.

G. Parietal bone (top of the head).

To strike with a brick on body parts in the sequence mentioned here. To strike on every body parts strictly **three blows,** no more no less. Striking force is moderate – not too weak and not too strong (detailed description of training methods and specific recommendations will be given below).

7. It is necessary to concentrate your attention on a trained region and see with due attention to the exactness of movements

Absolute exactness is required during a training session, one must not commit the slightest negligence. In order to attain exactness in movements, it is necessary to look attentively at a struck body part and it also is necessary to see to the proper position of an arm that holds a brick. Your attention must be concentrated on the exercise without diverting it even for a second. Negligence can do harm and that contradicts to training aims.

8. During the whole practice of PAI DA GONG it is not allowable:

a. To have sex. It is the most important requirement, it allows keeping oneself clean and preserving the functional resources of the body. Otherwise it is even not worth starting to exercise in that kind of GONG FU.

b. To break the principle of continuity of the training process. Training continuity and regularity are important for any kind of GONG FU, but especially for that one. It is very important.

c. To deliver blows with different force – now stronger, now weaker. When you deliver blows at different parts of the body the force of blows must differ depending on the condition

of muscles and bones of the trained region. A trainee himself adjusts the force of blows depending on his physical conditions. However, blows at the same place must not be struck with different force at different time. The force of blows must be constant, it is to be increased very gradually. Haphazard actions will be of no use.

d. To consume alcoholic drinks to excess. It is more difficult to control one's conduct after drinking alcohol and sexual excess often happens at that. That is absolutely unacceptable for this kind of GONG FU.

Description of the Technique of Consecutive Blows at Different Body Parts

1. Arms

Lower part of the arms – forearms (from the elbow to the wrist).
A spot to be struck is the inner part of a forearm.

TRAINING METHOD:

Come close to a table and take a stand at a distance of one step from its edge. Training starts from your left arm. Take a step with your left leg toward the table so that the left foot be on an imaginary line connecting two adjacent table legs. Bend the left knee, straighten the right leg, the distance between the feet should be one big step. So you have taken the left stance GONG BU. Clench the left hand into fist, lay the left forearm on the table, parallel to its edge. The inner part of the forearm and the center of the fist (on the palm side) face up, the back of the fist and the outer part of the forearm from the wrist to the elbow are pressed to the table surface. It is the initial training position. Blows will be struck on the inner side of the forearm, from the wrist to the elbow.

Take a brick by its side (longer part) with your right hand, the thumb being on the inner side, four other fingers – from the outer side. HU KOU (a part of the palm between the thumb and the forefinger) must be closely pressed to the side of the brick. Raise the right hand high above the head and strike at the inner part of the left forearm with the brick side. Then, raise the brick above your head once more and strike again. Do so three times – three blows totally. One must give a yell at the striking moment, strain the forearm and concentrate QI.

Master Guo Cui Ya is strengthening the left forearm according to PAI DA GONG.

Then, do the exercise for the right arm. In that case the right foot is near a table leg, the right leg is bent, the left leg is straight and drawn back (the right stance of GONG BU). Put the right arm on the table. The outer part of the right forearm, from the wrist to the elbow, is pressed to the table surface; the inner part of forearm faces up. Take a brick by its middle part with the left hand, raise it above the head and strike with the side of the brick at the inner side of the right forearm. All requirements are the same: three blows, yelling a blow number, straining the forearm at the striking moment.

Upper part of the arm – from the shoulder to the elbow.
A spot to be struck is the inner part of an arm, on the bicep side.

TRAINING METHOD:

After practicing forearms, proceed to strengthening upper parts of arms. The exercise, like that one in the previous case, is done at first for the left arm, then for the right one, the position GONG BU is also used. Below we shall describe the method PAI DA for the left arm (it is done in the same way for the right arm).

Take a stand near a table edge, take the left GONG BU. Keep the left forearm in the vertical position, clench the left hand into fist and turn it with the palm toward your face. Place the upper part of the left hand (from the elbow to the armpit) on the

table, with the bicep up. Lean the torso slightly back. Seize a brick by the middle of its side (exactly in the same manner like in the previous case) with the right hand firmly. Raise the brick above the head and strike with its side at your bicep. Strike three consecutive blows like it was done in the previous case. Then, lower the hand holding the brick. Now and later all requirements in respect to the timing of a yell, QI and inner effort are the same.

Elbow – the region between the forearm and the upper part of the arm.
A spot to be struck is muscles of the arm in the region of bending (above and below the elbow).

TRAINING METHOD:

Take the position GONG BU like that one in two previous cases, where the left leg is "bow" (drawn forward and bent) and the right leg is "arrow" (drawn back and straight). Press the left fist to your chest, put the left arm that is bent on the table so that fist, elbow and shoulder be in one horizontal plane. In that position the left fist with the side of the thumb is pressed to the left part of the chest, the palm is turned down, the back of the fist faces up, the whole arm with its inner side is pressed to the surface of the table.

Master Guo Cui Ya is practicing the left elbow according to the methods PAI DA GONG.

Muscles in the region of the crook of the arm (above and below the elbow) are the striking spot. Take a brick with your right hand like you did in previous cases. Strike with the side of the brick at muscles in the elbow region. As far as other points are concerned, training methods completely coincide with training methods of other parts of the arm as described above. Exercise according to those instructions. Then, take a step back with your left leg, take the stance "stand at attention", then take a

step forward with your right leg (toward the table). The right leg is bent ("bow"), the left one is straight ("arrow"). Bend the right arm and put it on the table. Practice according to the above outline: take a brick with your left hand and strike blows at the region of the right arm above and below the elbow.

2. Legs

The front part of the shin.
A spot to be struck is the front side of the shin,
from the ankle to the knee.

TRAINING METHOD:

After finishing the previous exercise, draw the right leg back and put it beside the left leg. Then, move the left foot to the left side at a distance of one step. Bend the left knee, straighten the right leg, turn the torso to the left an take the left stance GONG BU. Toes of both feet point forward and a little to the right, the face and the breast are directed forward (to the left in respect to the initial position).

Note: Earlier, while practicing your arms, you made a forward step toward the table; now, while practicing legs, you make a

step to the left (to practice the left leg), then a step to the right
(to practice the right leg); so you stand sidewise to the table.

Hold the brick by two of its butts (on the side of short edges)
with both hands: your thumbs are from above, the other fingers
are from below. HU KOU (a part of palms between thumbs
and the forefingers) must be closely pressed to butt ends of the
brick. Raise the brick above your head, lower it and strike with it
on the front part of the left shin. Then, raise the brick again and
strike again. Do so three consecutive times. Similar to all other
cases, yell out a blow number, strain muscles of the shin,
concentrate your attention and direct QI to the region which is
practiced.

The front part of the hip.
A spot to be struck is the front side of the hip,
from the hip joint to the knee.

TRAINING METHOD:

Hip practicing is done after practicing the front side of the shin
of the same leg. From the position of the previous exercise, the
left GONG BU, turn your toes to the right and bend your
knees. At that time the chest and the face also turn to the right.
Thus, from the position of GONG BU you come to the
position MA BU. You face the table again. Take a brick with
both hands by two of its butts like you did in the previous
exercise, raise it above your head and strike with the lower

surface of the brick at the left hip. Strike three consecutive blows.

Master Guo Cui Ya is exercising the front part of his hip according to the method PAI DA GONG.

Note: Above consecutive practicing of the left leg is described, first the front part of the shin, then the front part of the hip. After it (from the position MABU), turn your toes to the right and take the right stance of GONG BU (with the left side toward the table). Practicing of the right leg is done in the same sequence. At first, strike three blows at the front part of the

shin, then make a turn (to face the table) to the left and take the stance MA BU. After that, strike three blows at the right hip. All general requirements are the same. With this, leg practicing is over.

3. Chest

Left and right parts of the chest.
Struck spot is chest muscles in the region of nipples.

TRAINING METHOD:

You finished the previous exercise (leg training) in the position MA BU. Straighten both legs and stand erect, at that time feet remain in their places; the distance between them is one step as before. Training posture: straight knees, toes pointed forward, straight torso. Take a brick by two of its butts with both hands, stretch your arms forward in front of the chest. Bending both arms and drawing elbows back and to sides, strike three times with the face surface of the brick on the left side of the chest, than three times on the right side. Slightly throw out your chest.

Note: First you exercise the left side of the chest, then the right one, strike three blows on each side. When you strike on the left part, move slightly forward the left side of the chest and draw the right side a little back. When you strike on the right side of

秘 練
訣 功

the chest, move slightly forward the right side and on the contrary draw the left side of the chest a little back. Strike on each side of the chest neither more nor less than three blows.

Master Guo Cui Ya is exercising his chest according to the method PAI DA GONG.

秘　練
訣　功

4. Both Body Sides

Left and right body side.
Struck spot is lower ribs a little above the waist level.

TRAINING METHOD:

The position of legs and the body is similar to that one in the previous exercise. Start from the left side. Clench the left hand into fist and raise it above your head. Tilt the torso a little to the right. Take a brick by its butt end with the right hand (it is necessary to choose a sufficiently long brick). The thumb is on the inner side of the brick and the other four fingers are on the outer side. Press the palm close to the butt of the brick. Draw the right hand holding the brick to the right at the level of the waist, then strike with the brick with all the might on the left side (the brick moves in the horizontal plane). Stick out the left side a little toward the blow at that moment and tilt the torso a little to the right. After the blow the right hand holding the brick returns to the initial position for the second blow. It is necessary to strike altogether three blows.

Then, strike in the similar way on the right side. For that purpose, raise the right fist above the head, take a brick with the left hand and strike blows on the right side from the left to the right in the horizontal plane with all the might. Stick out the right side a little to the right (toward the blow) at the striking

moment and tilt the torso a little to the left respectively. Like in case of the left body side, strike three blows on the right side.

5. Body Back

Struck spot is the upper part of the back (a little below shoulder-blades) on the body centerline.

TRAINING METHOD:

The initial position of legs and the torso is as in the previous exercise. Lean forward from that position so that the back lie in the horizontal plane and point upward. Raise your head, draw your shoulders back and cave in the back. Hold the brick by its butts with both hands, draw your arms to your back and straighten them. Raise the brick above the back and lower it with force on that part of the back that is exercised (on the centerline, a little below shoulder-blades).

At the striking moment thumbs will touch the back, other fingers will be on the top, palms are turned inside, facing each other.

Straighten your arms after the blow and bring them to the initial position, then strike again. Strike altogether three times.

6. Stomach

Struck spot is a little low the navel on the centerline of the body.

TRAINING METHOD:

After the execution of the previous exercise leg position does
not change. Straighten the torso and stand erect. Take a brick by
its long sides with both hands (both thumbs is on the upper side
of the brick and the other eight fingers are on the bottom side),
press your palms to side edges closely. Hold the brick so that
one of its butts be turned to the stomach and the other one
forward (one of the planes of the brick is above, the other is
below). Strike at the stomach a little bit below the navel with the
butt of the brick three times. Concentrate QI in the lower part
of the stomach and stick out the stomach toward the blow a
little. Count the number of blows loudly. At that time as it was
earlier a blow and a yell must be at the same time.

7. Upper Part of the Head

Struck spot is the upper part of the frontal bone between the hair line (on the front) and the head crown.

TRAINING METHOD:

After finishing the previous exercise, bring the left leg close to the right one and stand erect with heels in, toes out (feet in the shape of hieroglyph "BA" - "/\"). Take a brick by its butt ends with both hands, thumbs inside, the other fingers outside, press HU KOU (of the palm) close to the butt ends of the brick. Raise the brick above your head on stretched arms (one of the brick planes up, the other down), bend your arms and strike with the lower plane of the brick on the upper part of the head between the forehead and the crown. Raise the brick again and strike once more. Strike altogether three blows. Clench your teeth tightly, count blows loudly, concentrate your attention on the practiced region. With this training according to the method PAI DA GONG is over.

Training Method of External Hard GONG FU from the Book "Canon on Transformation of Muscles and Tendons" (YI JIN JING)

Lately training methods from treatise "Canon on Transformation of Muscles and Tendons" are being widely spread and advertised. Illustrated booklets about those method are sold in many provinces and districts to make it possible to exercise by pictures. Although the material does not contain many details, it is sufficiently clear and easy to understand. Those booklets are usually titled as "External GONG FU for Transformation of Muscles and Tendons", "Illustrated Training Method for External GONG FU" and so on. It is usually stressed that training exercises must be done in a quiet place, facing the wall, calmly and with concentration. One must not overstrain the body, as the exercises cause QI inflow to arms and excess muscle strain hinders free flow of QI. Therefore, in case of excess muscle strain arms are not filled with QI

properly. Being in one of twelve positions, you must count to yourself up to 49, then, without stopping, proceed to the next position. Start acquiring the first position; then, having acquired it, add the second one and so on. After half a month or one month at most you will acquire all positions and then strength will gradually fill your whole body from feet to the head crown. This kind of training is intended to increase physical strength LI and fill the body with QI, as well as for strengthening the muscular system. However, to attain really profound results, one must seriously observe the ban for alcohol and sex, exercise 5-7 times daily (each day without interruption) and eat 4-5 times daily.

If a man exercises during 100 days, his physical strength increases by 1000 JINs[14]. It applies to young and strong people. The strength of a weaker man may increase, say, by 500 JINs. And if an old enfeebled man exercises in that manner only 2-3 times daily, he can improve his health and make his life longer. No illness will be passed to him. Really, it is beyond of understanding how effect of those training is so wonderful and miraculous.

Editor's notes:

[14] 1000 JINs are approximately equal to 500 kg, or 1100 lb (a figure of speech).

Jin Yi Ming, Guo Cui Ya. LIAN GONG MI JUE:
Secret Methods of Acquiring External and Internal Mastery (Shanghai, 1930)

秘 練
訣 功

12 Positions of the Method YI JIN JING

Jin Yi Ming, Guo Cui Ya. LIAN GONG MI JUE:
Secret Methods of Acquiring External and Internal Mastery (Shanghai, 1930)

秘 練
訣 功

Position one

Face east, look forward, set feet aside to shoulder width, parallel each other. Arms are lowered along the body, elbows are a little bent, the backs of hands face up and palms down. Fingers are locked with each other and stretched out parallel to the ground, fingertips point forward and a little bit upward. Start counting to yourself from 1 to 49. With each count raise fingertips a little bit more up and lower a palm a little down[15]. During intervals between counts relax hands a little and bring them to the initial position. "Lower" and "raise" 49 times in such a manner.

Editor's notes:

[15] Here the physical movement is practically unnoticeable; it has rather a meaning of "internal effort".

Position one

Position two

After finishing the first exercise, without changing position, clench all fingers except thumbs into fists. Turn the backs of fists forward, straighten thumbs inward, almost touching side surfaces of hips with them. Count from 1 to 49 in the same way, with every count clench fists stronger and try to raise the tips of thumbs still higher (fists remain at their place at that time). Clench fists and raise thumbs 49 times in such a manner.

Position two

Jin Yi Ming, Guo Cui Ya. LIAN GONG MI JUE:
Secret Methods of Acquiring External and Internal Mastery (Shanghai, 1930)

Position three

After finishing the second exercise, without changing the position, bend thumbs toward the centers of palms and clench the other fingers into fists (the thumb is pressed to the palm and grappled with four fingers from above). Straighten arms. Turn HU KOU[16] forward. With every count clench fists, during intervals between counts slightly relax. Count to 49 in such a manner.

Editor's notes:

[16] HU Kou, lit. "Tiger mouth", here and after a space between the thumb and forefinger.

Position three

Position four

After finishing the third exercise, without changing the position of legs and the torso, raise arms forward in front of the breast to the horizontal position. Stretch fists[17] forward at the shoulder level. Bend elbows a little, turn HU KOU up, the distance between fists must be a little more than 1 CHI (33 cm, or 1.094 ft). Press fists with every count stronger. Count to 49.

Editor's notes:

[17] Here and further in the text nothing is said about a change in methods of fist clenching; probably, thumbs remain clenched in fists.

Position four

Jin Yi Ming, Guo Cui Ya. LIAN GONG MI JUE:
Secret Methods of Acquiring External and Internal Mastery (Shanghai, 1930)

Position five

After finishing the fourth exercise, without changing the position of legs and the torso, stretch arms up, turn HU KOU back. Arms must not touch the head (they must be placed vertically). As before, fingers must be clenched into fists. Count to 49 as before, clenching fists stronger with each count.

Position five

Jin Yi Ming, Guo Cui Ya. LIAN GONG MI JUE:
Secret Methods of Acquiring External and Internal Mastery (Shanghai, 1930)

Position six

After finishing the previous exercise, without changing the position of legs and the torso, lower arms in front of you at the shoulder level, bend elbows and turn them to sides, turn down HU KOU of both fists with palms forward. Fists must be at the distance of 1 CHI (33 cm, or 1.094 ft) from each other. Clench fists with each count; at the same time, move elbows a little bit back[18] with force. Do so 49 times.

Editor's notes:

[18] Here as before, the physical movement can hardly be seen, it is rather "internal" effort.

Position six

Position seven

After finishing the previous exercise, without changing the position of legs and the torso, stretch out arms to sides at the shoulder level, turn fist HU KOU up. Shift body weight to heels; toes slightly lose contact with the ground; clench fists with force and raise them a little bit up. Lower toes to the ground, unclench fists slightly. Do so 49 times, count from 1 to 49.

Position seven

Jin Yi Ming, Guo Cui Ya. LIAN GONG MI JUE:
Secret Methods of Acquiring External and Internal Mastery (Shanghai, 1930)

Position eight

After finishing the previous exercise, without changing the position of legs and the torso, stretch out arms forward at the shoulder level. Everything is like in the fourth position, merely arms are completely straightened in elbows and the distance between fists is 5-6 CUNs (16,7-20,0 cm, or 6,6-7,9 in). Clench fists with every count. Count to 49.

Position eight

Jin Yi Ming, Guo Cui Ya. LIAN GONG MI JUE:
Secret Methods of Acquiring External and Internal Mastery (Shanghai, 1930)

Position nine

After finishing the previous exercise, bend elbows, draw fists to your nose with palms turned inside. The distance from the nose to the backs of fists must be 2-3 CUNs (6.6-9.9 cm, or 2.6-3.9 in). Count from 1 to 49, clenching fists with each count.

Position nine

Jin Yi Ming, Guo Cui Ya. LIAN GONG MI JUE:
Secret Methods of Acquiring External and Internal Mastery (Shanghai, 1930)

Position ten

After finishing the previous exercise stretch out arms to sides at the shoulder level, bend elbows and place forearms vertically, point HU KOU to ears. Arms and the head form the hieroglyph "SHAN": 山. Clench fists with each count, raising them a little up and moving elbows forward hardly noticeably. Do it 49 times.

Position ten

Jin Yi Ming, Guo Cui Ya. LIAN GONG MI JUE:
Secret Methods of Acquiring External and Internal Mastery (Shanghai, 1930)

Position eleven

After finishing the previous exercise, lower your fists with palms turned inside to the navel. Forefingers must be on the navel level, the distance between them must be 2-3 CUNs (6.6-9.9 cm, or 2.6-3.9 in). Clench fists with each count, count to 49.

Position eleven

Jin Yi Ming, Guo Cui Ya. LIAN GONG MI JUE:
Secret Methods of Acquiring External and Internal Mastery (Shanghai, 1930)

After finishing the eleventh exercise, relax muscles and make three cycles of deep breath, it is necessary to breathe with the lower part of the stomach.

Position twelve

After breathing in and breathing out deeply three times, lower your arms along the body, open your hands, straighten fingers, raise arms in front of you to the shoulder level, tiptoe at the same time. Imagine that you carry a heavy weight on your shoulders. Make the movement three times. Then, relax arm muscles by raising arms three times above the head and lowering them freely along the body. Then, shake each leg three times, starting with the left leg. Put feet at shoulder width. That is the end of the exercises complex.

Position twelve

Jin Yi Ming, Guo Cui Ya. LIAN GONG MI JUE:
Secret Methods of Acquiring External and Internal Mastery (Shanghai, 1930)

After finishing training according to the method YI JIN JING it is recommended to do several free and relaxed steps. If a middle-aged man, weak and unhealthy, exercises according to those methods, only after few months he will enjoy life and become cheerful and vigorous. He will feel that all his diseases will have abated. A lot of the credit must go to the wonderful method YI JIN ING that is very useful for people's health.

BA DUAN JIN
Eight Pieces of Brocade.
Ancient Method of Health
Improvement Composed
of Eight Exercises

The ancient method "Eight Pieces of Brocade" (BA DUAN JIN) is an excellent method for body perfection and health improvement. The author of the book used it in his childhood: the exercises are not complicated, easy to acquire and do. It is possible to obtain quick and tangible results through that method into the bargain. In the course of centuries-old history many things were lost, but the method BA DUAN JIN was preserved up to this day. It is so simple and easy to do that even women and children practice it. Below we shall present the training method BA DUAN JIN. Besides excellent health improvement the method develops motive skills which are required for martial arts. Undoubtedly, it is one of the best methods to exercise GONG FU.

1. Support the sky with both arms to adjust three SAN JIAO[19]

Stand erect with feet on the shoulder width. Raise both arms above the head, turn the hands with the palms up, couple fingers of both hands. Stretch out arms upward, raise your heels a little (tiptoe), take a deep breath at the same time. Bring arms down slowly in front of you and lower the heels to the ground while breathing out. Do that movement eight times.

2. Draw the bow to the left and right as if you shoot at an eagle

Set feet to the left and to the right so that the distance between them to be two CHIs approximately (about 0.67 m, or 2.2 feet). Take the stance MA BU: hips are situated horizontally, knees are bent, shins are perpendicular to the ground, the torso is straight. Bend both arms in front of the chest, palms are joined with each other at the shoulder level. Move slowly the left hand to the left at the shoulder level, the forefinger being straightened

---

Editor's notes:

[19] "Three Heaters" (SAN JIAO) in Chinese traditional medicine is a conventional organ that combines the functions of several organs. The upper heater summarizes the functions of the heart and the lungs in the distribution of QI and blood for nourishment of different organs and tissues. The middle heater summarizes the functions of the spleen and the stomach in digestion and absorption of nutrients. The lower heater summarizes the functions of the kidneys and bladder, controls water exchange and secretions.

and pointing up, the other fingers are bent. Concurrently with the movement of the left arm to the left, clench the right hand into fist and move it to the right. The right arm remains to be completely bent in elbow, the right hand stops near the right shoulder. The left arm moves to the left until it is completely straightened in elbow, the forefinger points up. The movement looks as if you draw the bow. It is necessary to closely watch the movement of the left forefinger. While "drawing the bow", breathe in; while "shooting an arrow" (returning arms to the initial position in front of the chest), breathe out. Then, stretch out the right arm to the right side at the shoulder level, concurrently move slowly the left arm that is bent in front of the chest at the shoulder level from the right to the left as if you draw the bow. Move your eyes to follow the right forefinger. Do this exercise eight times to each side.

3. Raise each arm separately to adjust spleen and stomach

Bring the left arm down along the body, straighten fingers and direct them forward with the palm facing the ground. Raise the right arm vertically up, straighten fingers and point them back with the palm facing up. Both arms are straight, the palms as if slightly push something, one (left) palm moves down, the other (right) one moves up. Breathe in at that time. Bring the right arm down, breathe out at that time. Then, stretch out the left arm up and the right one down, breathe in at that time. Raise and bring down arms in turn; each arm must be raised eight times.

4. Look backward to eliminate "five indispositions" and "seven damages"[20]

Take a stand "at attention" (heels in, toes out), legs are straight, bring arms down along the body, press palms to hips. Turn slowly the head to the left. Look back over the left shoulder. Breathe out at that time. Return slowly the head to the initial position, look straight forward. Breathe in at that time. Turn slowly the head to the right. Look back over the right shoulder. Breathe out at that time. During the exercise the torso does not move, only the head turns. One must try to turn the head back as far as possible. Turn the head eight times to each side.

5. Shake the head, wag the tail to extinguish fire in the heart

Put feet to sides at the length of one step, take the stance MA BU. Place palms on knees so that thumbs be on the outer sides of hips and the other fingers on the inner sides. Lean slowly the torso and the head to the left; bend the left arm a little bit at that time, the right arm remaining to be straight. Then, lean slowly the torso and the head to the right, bend the right arm a little bit and straighten the left arm completely in elbow. Keep

---

Editor's notes:

[20] "Five indispositions" are diseases of five internal organs: heart, liver, lungs, spleen, and kidneys; "seven damages" are damages of internal organs caused by excess emotions.

the back and head straight, do not bend the neck. Do eight leans to each side.

6. Shake seven times and one hundred diseases vanish

Bring your arms down along the body, press palms to hip sides. The torso and legs are straight. Join feet (heels and toes in). Tiptoe slowly, then bring heels down to the ground. Do so seven times. Keep the torso and the head vertically. Due to it you can increase the strength and resilience of muscles and tendons and get rid of many diseases.

7. Clench fists, cast fierce look, increase your power with QI

Collect your strength, sink into the position MA BU. Clench both fists and bring them to the sides near waist, elbows are bent and point back. Raise the right fist to the chest and deliver a straight blow to the right at the shoulder level, turn the fist with the HU KOU upward. Look fiercely in the direction of the blow. Return the right fist to the waist. Make the similar movement to the left side with left fist. While striking, breathe out; while returning the fist to the waist, breathe in. Make eight blows to each side.

Jin Yi Ming, Guo Cui Ya. LIAN GONG MI JUE:
Secret Methods of Acquiring External and Internal Mastery (Shanghai, 1930)

8. Hold your feet with both hands to strengthen kidneys and waist

Take the stance "at attention" (feet in). Bend your waist and lean forward and down. Keep your legs straight, on no account bend them. Stretch down your arms as low as possible. It might be as well to catch toes of feet with hands. It is a matter of some difficulty for many at the start, but gradually, in four or five days, you will be able to reach toes. If you do this exercise in a regular way, it will improve condition of your kidneys and waist; furthermore, it will slenderize you, maintain your straight spine and eliminate its curvature. This exercise must also be done eight times.

That is the end of the exercising complex according to the method BA DUAN JIN.

秘 練
訣 功

The studies of available historical documents did not reveal definitely either the originator of the method BA DUAN JIN or the time of its origination. Long ago Zhuang Zi[21] wrote that "breathing in and out", that is breathing exercises, or "removal of the spoiled and the intake of the fresh" in terms of Taoist teaching, promote health and long life. That statement was recorded in the collected works Zi Shu Bai Jia, or "Book of Philosophers of a Hundred of Schools". Zhuang Zi was one of the first scientists who made a scientific approach to health improvement. Later, the famous scientist and healer Hua Tuo[22] made a complex of exercises WU QIN XI, or "Frolics of The Five Animals" where movements of tiger, deer, bear, monkey, and crane are imitated. The idea was to improve health by imitating behavior and movements of animals. Hua Tuo said that the human body must be subjected to moderate physical loads, which promote blood and QI circulation and improve health. In that case diseases can not penetrate the human body. As a proverb says, "no stagnation in running water, no worm in the door hinge". In case of some diseases Hua Tuo prescribed to a

---

Editor's notes:

[21] Zhuang Zi (369-286 B.C.), a prominent representative of ancient philosophic Taoism.

[22] Hua Tuo (141? - 208) is a famous physician and a follower of Taoism. Lived at the end of the dynasty Eastern Han. Was the first physician to use narcosis and anesthesia for surgery. Besides, he created a complex of "Plays of Five Animals" (WU QIN XI) owing which through the imitation of movements of different animals - bear, tiger, deer, monkey, and crane the energy Qi properly circulates in a human organism and that cause effects of rejuvenation and invigoration.

Jin Yi Ming, Guo Cui Ya. LIAN GONG MI JUE:
Secret Methods of Acquiring External and Internal Mastery (Shanghai, 1930)

patient a certain complex of movements that imitated behavior of one of the five animals. Certain movements and postures cause the inflow of QI to certain organs and parts of the body, thus producing therapeutic effect. BA DUAN JIN that originates from methods Zhuang Zi and Hua Tuo is based on the same principles. It is a time-tested recipe for health and long life. Its deep and soft movements are in full conformity with physiological requirements of the human body.

I call upon westernized men not to treat their own heritage with contempt. We must advertise our national culture. It will promote the health of the nation and allow us to advance alongside of Eastern and Western powers.

Jin Yi Ming, Guo Cui Ya. LIAN GONG MI JUE:
Secret Methods of Acquiring External and Internal Mastery (Shanghai, 1930)

QING GONG

Art of Lightness: the Development of Ability for High and Long Jumps.

High jumps over a tree

High jumps over a tree are exercised stage by stage with certain exercises to be used at each stage. At first, it is necessary to choose a small tree. Each day, at fixed time, it is necessary to jump over the tree several times. One must exercise every day without stopping training process. Your results will grow with tree growth. Of course, at the start the tree is too small, it is easy to step it over; it may seem that such kind of training is of no value. However, if you join your feet or place them parallel at a small distance and try to jump over a tree using only effort of your ankles and pushing off with toes without bending knees (your legs remain fully straight in knees), you will feel that the task is far from being easy. On the other hand, when the tree will grow to the height of your breast or shoulders it will be difficult to jump it over without running even if you bend your legs in knees. Therefore, exercising in high jumping is conducted stage by stage and different techniques and methods are used at every stage. Below we shall explain those methods one by one in detail for the reader to be able to acquire them.

1. Method of Jumping Over a Small Tree
with Straight Legs

High jumping with straight legs is the base of further whole training. During the initial stage it is the best to exercise by a burgeoning sprout that is not higher than 1 CUN (3.3 cm, or 1.312 in). Although it is a tiny tree, it grows from day to day. If you exercise tirelessly your mastery will increase with the growth of the tree. The training method is as follows. Take a stand in front of the sprout, join feet or place them at the distance of 2-3 CUNs from each other (6.6-10 cm, or 2.6-3.9 in). Your legs are straight, do not bend knees. Toes point forward. Concentrate force in your toes, raise your heels a little. Keep your arms along the body sides. Jump over the tree a few times, maintaining your legs straight (without bending knees).

This method of high jumping greatly differs from high jumping with bent legs or from running jumps. There is a great difference between them. For example, if you jump with bent legs (from the squatting position) you can jump over an obstacle of 1 CHI (33.3 cm, or 1.094 feet) high, but you can take only the height of 1 CUN (3.3 cm, or 1.312 in), jumping with straight legs. And if you make a running jump you can jump over even an obstacle of 3 CHIs high. Exercising in high jumps with bent legs or running jumps yields results in CUNs and exercising with straight legs only in FENs[23]. If the result with straight legs

---

Editor's notes:

[23] 1 CUN = 10 FENs.

increases by 1 FEN, the result with bent legs increases by 1 CUN. It is explained by the work of powerful hip muscles in the process of unbending; besides, the body acquires kinematical energy. In the process of jumping with straight legs everything depends only upon the strength and elasticity of muscles of calves (gastrocnemii) and tendons. That's why high jumping with straight legs is an indispensable exercise that lays foundation of success in future. This method must be diligently and assiduously practiced. One must not feel disappointment and stop exercising in the face of a seemingly insignificant and slow increase in results.

Jin Yi Ming, Guo Cui Ya. LIAN GONG MI JUE:
Secret Methods of Acquiring External and Internal Mastery (Shanghai, 1930)

2. Method of Jumping over a Tree with Leg Bending

As it was noted before, high jumping with straight legs is a base for further whole training. Progress in this exercise is attained slowly and the time comes when the small tree will grow to a height unattainable for you if you jump with straight legs. Usually that moment comes when the height of the small tree approaches the knee level. In that case it is necessary to proceed to the next training stage, which is jumping with bent legs.

Take a stand in front of the small tree at a distance that is a little longer than 1 CHI (33.3 cm, or 1.094 feet). Place feet close to each other, bend your legs in knees. Bring both arms back quickly, tilt the torso forward at the same time (the face and the breast will be above the tree), raise the heels above the ground, push off with toes with force and jump over the top of the tree. At the time of jumping your arms are thrust forward and upward with force, your legs are being bent in knees, your feet are flying over the top of the tree. Land on the front parts of feet with your back facing the tree (at that moment the distance between feet must not exceed 2-3 CUNs (6.6-10 cm, or 2.6-3.9 in)). It is necessary to bend your legs in knees and squat at the landing moment. Then, turn about (facing the tree) and make a new jump. This exercise must be done daily, two times a day – in the morning and in the evening. It is necessary to make a certain number of jumps each time. Your result will increase with the growth of the tree.

3. Method of Running Jumps over a Tree

Running jumps over a tree is the next stage of training in high jumping. It is that kind of training that most of the people incautiously like, as the effectiveness of running jumping is much higher than jumps without running: trainees enjoy high results. However, one must keep in mind that "high result" here is actually attained due to kinematical energy accumulated by the body while running. Therefore, in a sense, it is an illusory result, while a standing jump is a real one. As a proverb goes, "it is easy to have illusions but it is difficult to find the truth". Therefore one must not ignore the first two stages. Only when the tree becomes higher than man's height one may proceed to running jumps.

The training method for running jumps is as follows. Take a stand facing a tree at the distance of 2-3 ZHANGs (6.6-10 m, or 7.3-10.9 yd) from it. There must be no any obstacles or extraneous objects on the patch between you and the tree. Run quickly toward the tree, bend your arms a little in elbows, clench hands into fists, swing arms forward and backward, everything like in usual running. Having reached the tree, push off with force from the ground and fly up. The left leg is brought forward, the right leg follows it. Having jumped over the tree, land on both feet at the same time, the distance between feet must be 3-4 CUNs (10-13.3 cm, or 3.9-5.3 in). Bend legs in knees at the landing moment and squat a little, press fists to your waist with palms up at that time and direct elbows back. If landing is not correct enough, make a step forward or backward immediately to restore balance. Exercise in the above-mentioned manner and you will get a good result. Here the

success fully depends on trainee's zeal. If you can not jump over the tree yet, you can cut off its top and continue exercising. But we would like to remind you again – the matter is in trainee's diligence and zeal. You will make progress if you manifest persistence and doggedness.

Method of Jumping Over a Bamboo Barrier

As a matter of fact, jumping methods in that case do not differ from jumps over a tree; one jumps in the same way with straight legs, with bent legs or makes a running jump. The only difference is that a special construction, a bamboo barrier, is used as an obstacle. To arrange a barrier, take two bamboo sticks, 8 CHIs long (2.7 m, or 8.8 feet) and drill some number of holes at an equal distance from each other, like they do on a musical pipe. The distance between adjacent holes must be about 1 CUN (3.33 cm, or 1.312 in). Dig those bamboo sticks into the ground at the depth of 1 CHI (33.3 cm, or 1.094 feet) so that the sticks will be vertical and the distance between the sticks 6 CHI (2 m, or 6.5 feet). The sticks must be dug in so that the holes on both sticks will be directed to one side. Take then two bamboo pins and insert them into the holes on both sticks at an equal height. Take then a thin bamboo pole, 8 CHIs long, and place it on the bamboo pins. So, the arrangement has the shape of letter "H". The horizontal pole may be put at any height by changing the position of bamboo pins that can be higher or lower according to your abilities and jumping methods. This exercising method is safe and allows easy adjustment of the height of an obstacle at will. It is an excellent method to exercise high jumping.

Jin Yi Ming, Guo Cui Ya. LIAN GONG MI JUE:
Secret Methods of Acquiring External and Internal Mastery (Shanghai, 1930)

Method for Training in High Jumping from the Bottom of a Pit

High jumping from the bottom of a pit is of two kinds – direct jumps from the bottom of a pit and jumps from matting on the bottom of a pit. In the first case, it is necessary to dig a pit to a certain depth in accordance with the strength of your legs. Get upon the pit bottom, clench your hands into fists, put feet close to each other. Squat, summon your strength and jump up onto the brink of the pit; stretch out your arms forward at that moment. Jump down onto the pit bottom again, jump up again, etc. Do exercising each morning and evening. Dig your pit deeper gradually with the growth of your training level. Doing in this manner, your result will gradually become better.

In the second case matting is placed on the pit bottom, it is the best training method for high jumping with straight legs. Its efficiency exceeds training methods of jumping over a tree or a bamboo barrier. Dig a pit of required depth for exercising and put several layers of mats on its bottom. At the initial training stage the depth from the brink of the pit to the upper layer of mats must be a little more than 1 CUN (3.3 cm, or 1.312 in). Get upon the mat layer on the bottom of the pit, your legs fully straight, feet joined, your arms down along the sides, palms pressed to the hips. Concentrate force in the toes, tiptoe slightly and jump up (always keep your legs straight in knees!). Exercise several times each day, making several jumps each time. When you feel that the strength has increased, remove one mat and continue exercising. So, remove one mat in each 3-5 days. It is necessary to train yourself daily, never interrupting training.

When you remove the last mat, you may deepen the pit and continue training. With time success will come – you will be able to get to the roof of a house with a jump as easily as you walk on a flat surface.

Jin Yi Ming, Guo Cui Ya. LIAN GONG MI JUE:
Secret Methods of Acquiring External and Internal Mastery (Shanghai, 1930)

Training Method for Long Jumping

Find a flat spacious ground for training and dig a long and shallow pit at one of the ends of the ground. If you chose a site which is elongate in the east-west direction, dig a pit in its eastern side. The length of the pit depends on physical level of training of the man who exercises, the width of the pit is arbitrary and the depth is a little more than 1 CHI (33.3 cm, or 1.094 ft). Fill in the pit with sand, flush with its brink. The exercising includes the following: get on the western edge of the ground, facing the pit. Optimal distance between you and the pit is about 2 ZHANGs (6.6 m, or 7.3 yd). Clench fingers into fists, bend elbows, keep fists on the sides near the waist. Start running with your arms swinging to and fro. On running to the brink of the pit, push off with your feet with all your force and jump forward as far as possible, using running inertia. The right leg is brought forward, the left leg follows it. Land on both feet at the same time, the distance between feet at the time of landing is 3-4 CUNs (10-13.3 cm, or 3.9-5.3 in). Bend your knees, squat, move your fists forward. If the position after landing is shaky, one or two short forward jumps on bent legs (in a squatting position) may be made to restore balance. It is necessary to exercise in the above manner several times a day, each day without exception. The power of legs and jumping range respectively will gradually grow. If necessary, increase the length of the pit and continue exercising. If you exercise for three years you will get excellent results.

秘 練
訣 功

Pole Jumping

Recently many schoolboys have become keen on this kind of high jumping. The method is as follows: take a long pole, catch it by its upper end with your right hand (HU KOU faces the lower end of the pole), catch the pole with your left hand (HU KOU faces the upper end of the pole) a little lower than the right hand. The distance between the hands is about 2-3 CHIs (0.7–1.0 m, or 2.2-3.3 feet). Keep the pole in front of you so that its lower end to be below and a little to the left of you and its upper end above and a little to the right. Take a jump in such a manner: take a run, prop the lower end of the pole against the ground, raise your body to the air due to accumulated kinematical energy and, resting on the pole, go over the obstacle. At the moment of overcoming the obstacle your legs leave the torso behind, so they are in front and the torso behind. The hands that are squeezing the pole are a little to the left and behind the torso. Such kind of jumping is possible only with the aid of a pole. It is not considered an orthodox GONG FU, that's why a simplified description has been given.

Jin Yi Ming, Guo Cui Ya. LIAN GONG MI JUE:
Secret Methods of Acquiring External and Internal Mastery (Shanghai, 1930)

秘 練
訣 功

Art of Lightness: Training with Lead Plates

Training methods with lead plates is very simple. The trainee himself, taking into account his abilities and the power of his legs, selects lead plates of a certain weight. The plates must have a certain curvature so if applied to a shin, the whole inner side of the plate would touch it. Take then two cloth bands, 6-8 CHIs (2.0-2.7 m, or 6.6-8.8 ft) long and 3-5 CUNs (10.0-16.7 cm, or 3.9-6.6 in) wide, and wind several layers around the shin. Put then the plates with their concave sides to the cloth bands on the side of calves, wind the loose ends around the shin and fix the bands. The main requirement is as follows: the lead plates must be tightly fixed and must not hang loosely (move along the shin). Taking into account the above-said, adjust the degree of tightness of winding. In the morning, after getting up, wind the lead plates around to your shins and walk some distance. It is necessary to increase a little the distance to be walked. Increase the weight of the lead plates gradually, too. Do not remove the plates during your training sessions in high and long jumping! With time you will gain excellent results. If you remove the lead plates your results will increase by several times and you will feel unusual lightness in the whole body. Inexpressible joy will overwhelm you and it will seem to you that you are able to fly, hardly touching the ground. Undoubtedly, it is the best training method of QING GONG – "Art of Lightness".

Jin Yi Ming, Guo Cui Ya. LIAN GONG MI JUE:
Secret Methods of Acquiring External and Internal Mastery (Shanghai, 1930)

SOFT GONG FU
Exercises for Development of Flexibility of Muscles, Joints and Tendons

The soft Gong Gong Fu is an indispensable part of training in martial arts. First of all, it is necessary to practice flexibility and mobility of one's waist and legs. It is a key point in acquiring flexibility and agility of the whole body; just from that start the learning of any style of traditional Chinese martial arts. Dexterity and mobility are required to execute any movement and technique – attack, retreat, dodging, or striking. Any action demands flexibility and mobility. If the body is clumsy and legs slow, potentialities of body extremities can not be completely used for delivering blows. It is better to perfect the soft GONG FU in one's young years when bones are soft and muscles and tendons elastic. Grown-ups have less mobile joints, their bones become hard; that's why it is appreciably difficult to obtain required results. A grown-up needs to do hard work and make great efforts, that's why it is better to exercise since young years. Below is given a training procedure to acquire mobility and flexibility of the waist and legs.

Jin Yi Ming, Guo Cui Ya. LIAN GONG MI JUE:
Secret Methods of Acquiring External and Internal Mastery (Shanghai, 1930)

Procedure for the development of flexibility and mobility of the waist

The method of the soft GONF FU with the aim to increase waist flexibility comprises the following: put feet to the left and to the right at the distance of one step and raise your arms above the head. Incline the upper part of the torso back and bend your legs in knees a little. Remain in that position for some time and try to incline lower. So, slowly, waist flexibility and the mobility of the lower part of the spine are increased. One must exercise twice a day, in the morning and in the evening, and do the exercise several times. With time your hands will be able to reach the floor at some distance behind feet. At first insignificant sensations of pain can be felt in the region of the lower back and the stomach but with time they will vanish and you will make a noticeable progress in practicing. In the end you will be able to bend your waist back so that your hands will touch the floor at some distance behind your feet. Move gradually your hands nearer to feet. Some time later you will be able to grapple your ankles with your hands, keeping the legs straight in knees. At that time you will be able to push your head between your legs under the crotch and look forward. It may seem to an onlooker as if the man has no bones at all. Then, your hands must be set against the ground; you must raise your leg vertically up, bring feet to the ground behind your hands and draw yourself up. In that manner you have executed a back rollover. So, setting arms against the ground and carrying the legs above the head, one can go to and fro. The exercise is called "windmill". With that you will enjoy full success in training.

Practicing the waist in flexibility.

Jin Yi Ming, Guo Cui Ya. LIAN GONG MI JUE:
Secret Methods of Acquiring External and Internal Mastery (Shanghai, 1930)

Procedure for the development of leg flexibility and mobility

The procedure for the development of flexibility and mobility of legs consists of five parts:

1. Take a stand in front of a table, set your arms against your sides (thumbs back, the other fingers in front). Your elbows are directed to sides. Start from practicing your right leg, keep the left leg fully straight at that time; do not bend knees. Raise the right leg and place it with its heel on the edge of the table, the toe points up. Bend the upper part of the torso forward and try to reach the right knee with your breast. It is difficult to do that at the beginning; in addition, pain can be felt in the knee. That's why it is necessary to bend toward the knee easily and slowly, without excessive efforts. Exercise daily in the morning and in the evening. With time you will be able to touch the knee with your breast. Practice your left leg in the same manner: put the left leg with its heel on the edge of the table, point the toe up, support yourself on the straight right leg. Like in practicing the right leg, bend the upper part of the torso forward and try to reach the left knee with your breast. Pay attention to both legs which must be absolutely straight. Practice both legs in turn and after all you will obtain required result. Never stop practicing because of pain in muscles.

**Master Jin Yi Ming is doing an exercise for development of leg
flexibility.**

Master Jin Yi Ming is doing an exercise for development of leg flexibility.

2. Stand upright; heels in, toes out, legs straight, knees unbent. Raise your arms above your head; interlace fingers of both hands, palms up, thumbs outside (forward). Bend down; at that time your arms are also moved down, hands are turned with palms toward the floor, thumbs inside. Maintain your legs absolutely straight, knees unbent. Try to touch the floor with your palms. It is rather difficult to do it at first but with time muscles will acquire required flexibility. It is one of the positions from BA DUAN JIN.

3. Raising legs up. The purpose is the same as in two previous cases but the procedure is different. Before legs were in a static position and you tried to bring the upper torso to them as near as possible. Now, on the contrary, your torso is immovable (straightened) and legs must be raised as high as possible. With time you will be able to raise legs so high that the whole foot will be above the head. Get on the edge of the ground for training purpose, bend your arms in elbows and press your hands to the sides (thumbs behind, the other fingers in front). Your left leg takes a step forward; as soon as your left foot touches the ground, raise quickly your right leg in front of you as high as possible, the right leg being straight (the knee is not bent), the toe of the right foot being hooked (you pull the toe to the front side of the shin). Bring the right foot to the ground, the right foot only slightly touches the ground, half pace in front of the left foot; as before, body weight rests on the left leg. Immediately your right leg takes one more half pace forward; as soon as the right foot touches the ground, shift body weight to it and raise quickly the left straight leg in front of you as high as possible. Bring down the left foot in front of the right one and

so on. Exercise daily in the morning and in the evening. The result will be available after several months. With time you will be able to raise your legs so high that the foot will be above the head.

Master Jin Yi Ming executes the exercise "Splits in the shape of hieroglyph "One" (➖).

4. The splits in the shape of hieroglyph "one" (-). The exercise is composed of two parts - longitudinal splits and lateral splits. The longitudinal splits: straight legs, hands on the waist, one leg in front and the second one behind, try to touch the ground with your perineum. The lateral splits: bring legs to sides (to the right and to the left), try to touch the ground with your perineum and the inner side of legs. It is necessary to achieve that you should easily do both longitudinal and lateral splits and stand up from that position without aid of your arms – just to strain leg muscles and stand up. You must sit down and stand up without the aid of arms easily and freely. Certainly, pain will

be felt in legs at first and you will not manage without arms. Being in position "the splits", it is necessary to do right-left and to and fro bends with your torso while trying to touch your legs.

Method for the development of leg flexibility CHAO TIAN DENG – "Supporting the sky".

5. CHAO TIAN DENG – "To support the sky". The training process is difficult. First, it is necessary to acquire exercise "the splits" well, otherwise legs can not be raised to required height. While exercising one must be supported by one straight leg.

You raise the foot to the lower part of the stomach, catch the heel from below with your hand and raise the foot above the head. If the left leg rests on the floor, bend the right knee and raise the right foot to the level of the lower part of the stomach. Catch the right heel from below with your right hand and raise the right leg vertically above the head. The foot is on the right and a little in front as regard to the head; the toe points to the left, the sole faces the sky, the leg is straight, do not bend the knee. The right arm is slightly bent, the hand holds the heel. At that moment the left hand is rising up and catches the right toe. Practice the left leg in the same manner. With time you will be able to do the exercise easily. Some time later you will be able to do it without arms: one leg is on the floor, the other leg is rising up and stands vertically with its sole facing the sky. It is possible even to put a cup with water on the sole and try not to spill it.

Part II

NEI ZHUANG XING GONG

Method for Development of Internal Power

Method Description

Methods of GONG FU for the development of the External Power (WAI ZHUANG) are intended, first of all, for practicing extremities - arms and legs. Methods of GONG FU for the Internal Power (NEI ZHUANG) are intended for the protection and strengthening of "five dense organs" (WU ZANG: heart, liver, spleen, lungs, and kidneys) and "six hollow organs" (LIU FU: stomach, gall bladder, three heaters[24], urinary bladder, large intestine, small intestine). Method for practicing the External GONG FU are comparatively simple and those for the Internal GONG FU much more complicated, therefore most people are content with "external" methods and do not pay due attention to "internal" ones. That common and essential shortcoming is also explained by the fact that few people know true secrets of practicing the "internal" GONG FU. The people who sincerely wish to reach the heights of mastery must start from practicing the "internal" GONG FU and then proceed to the "external" one. The way of attaining mastery looks like growing a tree. Before planting a sapling one must loosen and manure soil and then carefully dig the roots into soil to suck nutrients and water from there. In that case its

---

Editor's notes:

[24] "Three Heaters" (SAN JIAO) in Chinese traditional medicine is a conventional organ that combines the functions of several organs. The upper heater summarizes the functions of the heart and the lungs in the distribution of QI and blood for nourishment of different organs and tissues. The middle heater summarizes the functions of the spleen and the stomach in digestion and absorption of nutrients. The lower heater summarizes the functions of the kidneys and bladder, controls water exchange and secretions.

trunk and branches will not wither and will grow and develop. Otherwise, though you even look after the trunk and branches well but have not fixed properly the root the best fertile soil and spring water will be useless. It might be said that NEI ZHUANG is a tree root and WAI ZHUANG is its trunk and branches. That's way it is necessary to start from the "internal" GONG FU and then, after strengthening the base, proceed to the "external" one. It will be difficult at first; on the other hand, it will be easy later on. It is a primary duty to look after the root of a tree and the branches will be luxuriant. Initially it is necessary to develop the "internal" power, NEI ZHUANG, then exercise the "external" power, WAI ZHUANG. Now we are going to say about methods for the development of the Internal Power.

It is best of all to start practicing at the beginning of a year, from the first or the second month[25], as blood and QI in spring are abundant and power and energy are on the rise. Besides, there is no risk to catch cold when you unbutton your clothes and bare some part of your body (for massaging). For exercising it is necessary to choose a quiet nook where nobody will disturb you and there are minimum external factors to distract. It is also necessary to invite four teenagers of 14-15 years old who will massage you. Youths of this age are full of energy and vitality, their QI is abundant, but at the same time they are comparatively weak from physical point of view, so massaging force will not too big.

Editor's notes:

[25] **Since February or March according to the European calendar.**

Get up early in the morning and take the drug (its recipe is given below), then for some time practice in YAN YE XI SUI – "Swallowing Ectoplasm, Rinsing Marrow" (the procedure is described in the next chapter). Within that time the drug will be dissolved in the stomach and starts to take its effect, after that one may proceed to massaging. Lie down on a bed or a couch, unbutton your outwear and ask one of your young assistants to stay on your right and put his palm in the region of your stomach between the heart and naval. Then rubbing (massaging) must be done from the right to the left slowly with short movements of moderate force. In the course of massage the hand of your masseur must not loose contact with your body, there must not be also relative movement between your skin and his palm (the palm must not glide over your skin but move together with it). That is the way to do massage. After the right arm is tired it is replaced with left arm, after one man is tired he is replaced with the second man. Don't indulge in idle thoughts and don't fall into daydreams during the massage. You must close your eyes and concentrate your attention on the palm of the masseur and the part of your body under his palm. Concentrate yourself on internal feeling and put aside external digressive factors. At the same time there is no need to overstrain your attention; you must be relaxed and quiet (both mentally and physically). Ideally, if you fall asleep while being massaged. After the end of a massage seance it is necessary to sit quietly. A massage seance lasts about one hour.

It is necessary to carry out three seances of massage every day - in the morning, at daytime and in the evening. If youths of twenty years old, physically strong and full of vitality, are at your service two seances per day are enough – in the morning and in the evening.

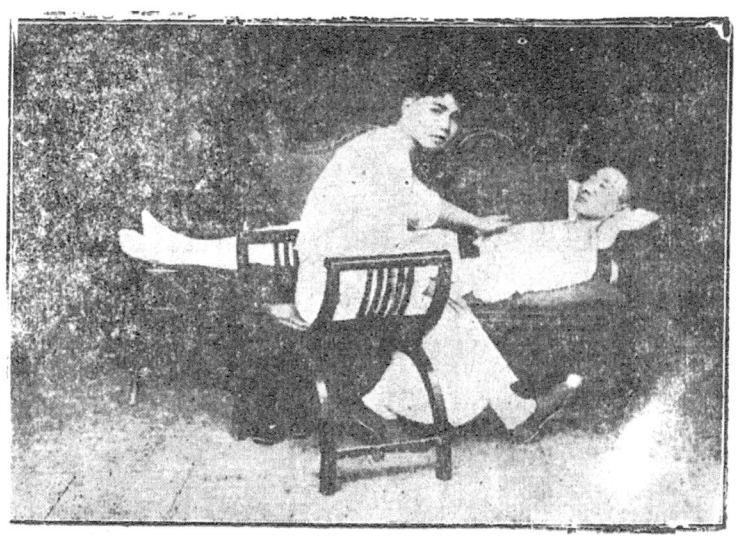

**Method for the development of the Internal Power: massaging
the front part of the body.**

Such massage must be carried out throughout the first month.
The result of the first month of practicing will be the
accumulation of QI in the region of your stomach. Additionally,
you will feel two tendons on the sides of your belly (on the left
and the right of your stomach) to become thickened and
distended (risen from the depth of your body to the surface),
they can be easily groped for. The width of each tendon is about
1 CUN (3.3 cm, or 1.312 in). If you strain them they are hard by
groping like wood. It proves that training during the first month
was right.

Now you must extend massaging place by the width of a palm
up and down from the "center", i.e. from the place where you
started massaging and continue massaging with the same

- 147 -

method like during the previous month. The part of the body between the solar plexus and the stomach is soft and sunken, as the diagram is under it. Above the diagram, under a layer of skin, are fascia, they are soft by touching. Usually manual massage is not strong enough to reach fascia, therefore a wooden mallet (pestle) wound with cloth is used. The mallet (pestle) is used to knead soft places and to strike light blows in order fascia to be made "swelled" and become hard like tendons on the sides of the stomach. You must reach such a state by the end of the second month of practicing.

During the third month the place under massage is increased by the width of one more palm, the procedure and requirements remaining the same. Now the region under massage lies from the breast bone to the waist and limited by rib ends on the sides. Kneading of fascia with palms and a mallet, rolling (with the mallet) and light blows are used. The purpose is the same – to make fascia hard and raise them to the surface of the body. During the fourth month results thus obtained are consolidated and improved. Massaging region lies from the breast bone to the waist, it is limited with rib ends on the sides. Rub with palms in the same manner, slap, knead with a mallet, then strike with a mallet. If by the end of the fourth training month tendons and fascia grow, become hard and rise to the body surface and the diaphragm (stomach region) is felt as bulged out it means that a good result has been obtained.

After four months of training the breast and stomach are filled with QI; fascia in the region of the stomach and abdomen are hardened and rise to the body surface. Five organs of ZANG and six organs of FU will be sound and strong. Now it is high time to divide NEI ZHUANG and WAI ZHUANG.

Accumulated QI should not go "outside", i.e. to body extremities and turn into "external power" but must enter bones, fill JING LUO[26], organs ZANG and FU. To that effect efforts must be concentrated during the period from the fifth to the eighth month of training, i.e. during next 120 days. As QI moves along the way of delivering blows (follows blows), it is necessary to do slaps and blows from the solar plexus toward the neck as well from rib ends outward on the breast toward shoulders. The sequence is as follows: massaging, slapping, and then striking. After finishing one cycle, proceed to the next one. Do not reverse the direction of blows; otherwise QI will not enter ribs. One must exercise in this manner for four months. As a result of it the breast and the whole front part of the body will be filled with QI. It is already more than a half of success.

The period from the ninth to twelfth month covers practicing the back. It is necessary to fill the rear part of the body – the back and the spine with QI at this stage. By that time QI has already reached shoulders and the neck and the task ahead is to spread it down the back. The same methods as before are used for that: rubbing (massage), slapping and striking (with a mallet). Blows are done from the side of the right shoulder from the neck to the point YU ZHEN[27], from the point YU ZHEN down, on soft tissues, to the point JIA JI [28], then down to the

---

Editor's notes:

[26] JING – "road", "path"; LUO – ""net", "cell"; JING LUO – a system of channels inside a human body where QI circulates.

[27] YU ZHEN , "Jade pillow", a point that is located opposite the occipital bone, on the central line of the body.

[28] JIA JI, lit. "narrow place", a point on the backbone between the sixth and seventh thoracic vertebras (opposite the heart).

point WEI LU (coccyx). Do massage and then strike in the above sequence. The same is done from the left part of the back. After finishing one cycle, proceed to the next one. Massage first, then strike. Direction of blows must not be reversed, do as indicated – from above downward. The number of training sessions per day and their duration remain the same. As a result of 120 days of exercising QI will fill the back and the spine; the back will become as strong as the breast. This is, in general outline, a method of the development of NEI ZUANG – the Internal Power.

秘 練
訣 功

Striking with a stick according to the method "Development of
internal power". Exercising with a stick can be carried out both
in lying and standing position. In the photo Fu Gong, thirteen
years old son of master Jin, strikes at the father's body with a
wooden stick wound in cotton fabric.

Recipe of a Drug for Internal Use Which Increases the Internal Power

When we speak about the Internal Power we, first of all, mean exercising aimed at making up the inborn deficiency, adjusting the balance between YIN and YANG of a human body as well as "rearing vitality". However, sometimes muscles and tendons massage alone is not enough to strengthen internal organs. Or it is necessary to obtain quicker and more tangible result. In that case drug exposure is supplemented by "external" methods. Those drugs must be taken early in the morning, immediately after getting up. When the drug is dissolved (in the stomach) and starts taking effect one may proceed to massaging. Thus, internal and external influences are put together and thanks to it one can get not only quicker and more significant effect but also to make up the inborn deficiency (in vitality). That is the essence of "making up" (deficiency in vitality) through drugs.

Drug composition: Ginseng, Bai Zhu (Atractylodes macrocephala), Dang Gui (Angelica sinensis), Chuan Xiong (Ligusticum chuanxiong), two FENs (756 mg, or 0.4266 dr) of each of the above-mentioned components. It is necessary to add to those ingredients wild-growing Bai Ji Li (Tribulus terrestris) without thorns, Bai Fu Ling (Pachyma cocos), Bai Shao Yao (Paeonia lactiflora, Chinese Peony), Di Huang (Rehmannia glutinosa), Gan Cao (Glycyrrhiza uralensis), Zhu Sha (Cinnabar), one QIANG (5 g, or 2.822 dr) of each component mentioned above. It is necessary to mix all those components,

grind to powder, add honey and make pills weighing 1 QIANG
(5 g, or 2.822 dr) each. If it is too expensive the weight of pills
may be decreased a little. When taking the pills, onion is
counter-indicative, as it is not compatible with honey.

One more recipe: Dang Gui (Angelica sinensis), Niu Xi
(Achyranthes bidentata var. japonica) soaked in vodka, Gou Qi
Zi (Lycium Chinese), Bao Jiao (fish bladder boiled soft) - 4
LIANs (200 g, or 7.056 oz) of each of the above-mentioned
components. Add to those ingredients wild-growing Bai Ji Li
(Tribulus terrestris) and crab yolk – 5 LIANs (250 g, or 8.82 oz)
of both. Bu Gu Zhi (Psoralea corylifolia) soaked in salt water,
HU TOU[29] - 4 LIANs of each of those components. It is
necessary to mix all those components, grind to powder, add
honey and make pills weighing 1 QIANG (5 g, or 2.822 dr)
each.

Pills prepared according to one of the above recipes must be
taken just before exercising, one piece each time, and washed
down with vodka. As practice showed, it gives a wonderful
result. Those pills are called miraculous and there are strong
grounds to believe that.

Editor's notes:

[29] HU TOU, lit. "tiger's head", probably old or local name of some plant,
medicine and etc.

Jin Yi Ming, Guo Cui Ya. LIAN GONG MI JUE:
Secret Methods of Acquiring External and Internal Mastery (Shanghai, 1930)

Innermost Essence and Importance of the Method XI SUI for Development of the Internal Power

YI JIN JING practice can increase physical power and strengthen the body of a practitioner and nothing more. Only the method "Rinsing marrow" (XI SUI) can make a man inspired. "External" training methods are only the initial stage on the way toward perfection and XI SUI actually is deep GONG FU. For successful practice in "Rinsing marrow" one must, first of all, have very serious intention and firm resolution. One must cast aside seven QING[30] and six YU[31], give up all vain desires, and leave behind anxiety about life and death. If you succeed in it you will get, after all, good results. At first it is difficult for a practitioner even to imagine all that but with time he starts to understand how to get success. You will be able disappear and appear, free yourself (from earthly passions) and reach the top of perfection. You will be flesh and blood; nevertheless, you will be able to fly freely like the wind[32].

Editor's notes:

[30] QI QING – seven feelings (emotions): joy (xi), anger (nu), sorrow (you), pensiveness (si), grief (bei), fear (kong), fright (jing).

[31] LIU YU – desires (lusts) which originate from six "roots": eyes, ears, nose, tongue, body, and brain.

[32] Buddhists believe that if a man can free himself from the bondage of emotions and desires his Spirit will become independent and will be able to leave the physical body and return to it at will.

Practiced methods do not look like methods of YI JIN JING, though achievements in YI JIN JING are used as a base (for XI SUI practice). Primordially "Canon on Rinsing Marrow" (XI SUI JING) was written in Sanskrit and later translated into Chinese. There is a xylographic edition; Buddhist monk Di Chen has one copy which I saw with my own eyes. It is a genuine Shaolin relic. However, the book contains a lot of special terms, notions and allegories based on the Buddhist teaching, therefore it is very difficult for a layman to understand and realize them so the book causes confusion and bewilderment in people. That is the reason why we are going to explain the essence of the method briefly and in understandable language.

It is necessary to cultivate high moral virtues and mind's stability in everyday life to obtain spiritual quietism. To get up every day early, before dawn. To face the sun, to breathe out three times, to sit down in Buddhist manner, turning the soles upward, to put hands on knees with palms facing up, to press the tongue tip to the palate. To turn mind's eye inward - to five organs ZANG and six organs FU. Not to see (not to look at) surroundings, to turn ear inward and hear how blood is circulating in the body. Not to hear (not to listen to) external sounds, breathe in and breathe out deeply. To breathe in and to breathe out slowly and smoothly, to swallow saliva. That is YAN YE XI SUI, the method of "Swallowing Ectoplasm and Rinsing Marrow".

Master Jin Yi Ming is practicing YAN YE XI SUI - "Swallowing Ectoplasm and Rinsing Marrow".

The above procedure YAN YE XI SUI is given in brief and may be not quite understandable due to it. However, it is necessary to keep in mind that who only reads (without practicing) will never understand how to do and who only practice (and who does not know proper methods) will never understand the importance of the method. Below we shall explain how "to go", "to stop", "to stand", "to sit", and "to lie". "Canon on Marrow Rinsing" (XI SUI JING) says that it is

necessary to go naturally, raise legs not high, to step slowly. When you has put down your foot and stand firmly on the ground the next step may be done. It can be said so about each step. Never be in hurry, as haste leads to mistakes. A moderate step affords safety. It is necessary to stop like a horse before the cliff, like a boat mooring to the coast. It is necessary to stand erect, never leaning, as to stand erect means to stand firmly. Nothing troubles eyes and ears, the heart is quiet like a mirror surface of water that reflects objects and events, not troubled by them. It is necessary to sit upright with quiet and serious face and the closed mouth, breathing through the nose. When QI is full the expression on the face is natural. Lie as follows: set your legs to sides, bend and raise your knees a little, crook toes, place your palms on the stomach. If you get tired, sleep on your side; when you wake up, stretch your legs and lie facing up for a while. In nine years you will see the result. You will not worry about problems of life and death. Methods of "going", "stopping", "standing", "sitting", and "lying" have significance in their own right; in addition, the methods give good auxiliary effect for practice XI SUI. However, not those methods serve as the foundation of XI SUI but the practice "Change of muscles and tendons" (YI JIN). If you practice YI JIN you will make your body as strong as diamond. It will seem to people that you are invulnerable. However, you are still in need of "dead" food and you are prone to "Seven passions". Although the body in outward appearance is as strong as diamond, all the same it consists of blood and flesh. Therefore it is necessary to practice "Rinsing marrow" and follow instructions of The Canon: to eat less, to breathe in fresh QI more, to take air-baths.

Get up at the hour of WU GENG[33]. Massage eyes, nose, mouth, and ears many times. You should look not further than the tip of your nose, your mouth is closed, breathe through nose. Do not spit out (saliva). Breathe out muddy QI and breathe in fresh QI. Do number one (to urinate). Do not be sleepy. Sit in the Buddhist way, prop the tip of your tongue against the hard palate, put your hand on knees with palms facing up, breathe smoothly, swallow saliva that appear in your mouth. Clatter your teeth for a while, then press with both hands in the region of the navel and make massage. Then stand up slowly and make a few steps without haste. Do not make fuss, as haste leads to mistakes. Everything should be done sedately and quietly. Calm your soul, put aside your passions and desires and you will become quite another man within three-nine years. You will stick to four "less": less talk, less anxiety in your heart, less food in your stomach, less sleep. It is those four "less" that assure long life. That's what secrets of the method "Rinsing marrow" are.

One can say that practicing of YAN YE XI SUI akin to "sinking into contemplation" (meditation) and preparation and taking potions belong to alchemy. It is considered that contemplation (meditation) and alchemy allow a man to attain the peak of perfection, envelop "the Sky and the Earth" and merge with them. Recently a lot of people call for the development of WU SHU" "without any prejudices". Even theories appear that the man can live long thanks to simple

---

Editor's notes:

[33] WU GENG, a time interval from 3 to 5 o'clock in the morning.

physical exercises. From the author's point of view, alchemy and meditation are inseparable from GONG FU and are its essence. It is stupid to deny the things which exist objectively. New theories must be based on new facts, not on the negation of existing ones. History has many evidences of it: a monk Da Mo (Bodhidharma) who sat facing a wall for nine years and sounds of ants became for him like thunder; Zhang San Feng, an alchemist from the Wudang Mountains who could be invisible and people thought him to be immortal. Before WU SHU became widespread people knew Da Mo only as the founder of the Buddhist school Sakyamuni (Gautama Buddha) in China but they did not know that he was the founder of the Shaolin School. San Feng also started his activities in Shaolin but then, having attained heights of the Teaching, he secluded himself in the Wudang Mountains; he is honored as the founder of the Wudang school. San Feng combined Taoist alchemy and methods of "contemplation" (meditation) of Chan Buddhism. As a matter of fact, different means and methods are a part of an entity. The author wrote this book on the base of many sources. I realize perfectly well that my knowledge in this field is far from being sufficient, pray to forgive my shortcomings and inaccuracies. I kindly ask for your commentaries and corrections. Thank you in advance.

The third decade of August, the 19-th year of the Chinese Republic (1930).

Jin Yi Ming from Yangzhou.

Shanghai, province of Jiangsu.

***

Jin Yi Ming, Guo Cui Ya. LIAN GONG MI JUE:
Secret Methods of Acquiring External and Internal Mastery (Shanghai, 1930)

Shaolin Kung Fu Online Library
www.kungfulibrary.com

Chinese Martial Arts - Theory & Practice
Old Chinese Books, Treatises, Manuscripts

Lam Sai Wing. Moving Along the Hieroglyph Gung, I Tame the Tiger with the Pugilistic Art.

Lam Sai Wing. Tiger and Crane Double Form.

Lam Sai Wing. TIET SIN: Iron Thread.

Jin Jing Zhong. Training Methods of 72 Arts of Shaolin.

Jin Jing Zhong. Dian Xue Shu: Skill of Acting on Acupoints.

Liu Jin Sheng. CHIN NA FA: Skill of Catch and Hold.

Tang Ji Ren. Pugilistic Art of the Tang Family. DA HONG QUAN.

Xu Yi Qian. CHUAN NA QUAN: Style of Piercing Blows and Holds.

Yuan Chu Cai. MEI HUA ZHUANG: Poles of Plum Blossom. External and Internal Training.